Especially for

_____

From

_____

On This Date

_____

Heavenly XOXO

Tender Tales and Inspiration to Warm Your Heart

BARBOUR
PUBLISHING

Cover and interior design: Thinkpen Design

Published by Barbour Publishing, Inc., P.O. Box 719, Uhrichsville, Ohio 44683, www.barbourbooks.com

Our mission is to publish and distribute inspirational products offering exceptional value and biblical encouragement to the masses.

Member of the
Evangelical Christian
Publishers Association

Printed in The United States of America.

Contents

Introduction

From the time we were children, many of us have signed our notes to loved ones with XOXO, the universal symbol for hugs and kisses. Those little letters take the place of a physical hug and kiss and remind the recipient of our ongoing tenderness and affection. They connect us. Bind us together. Offer a sense of nearness.

Those of us who walk closely with the Lord are aware of his supernatural XOXOs in our lives. Every day, in thousands of ways, He sends them our way. His heavenly hugs and kisses abound. We find them in a beautiful sunset or the dimples in a grandchild's cheeks. We sense them in the dewy morning, hear them sung in songs of praise on Sunday mornings. We witness them when someone extends a hand of blessing or forgiveness. In short, we're surrounded by the miraculous. The divine.

Oftentimes, though, we miss God's attempts to connect with us. We overlook His love gifts. We're simply not paying attention. Life's busyness has us distracted. Oh, but those heavenly XOXOs are there! Look around you. See beyond life's painful circumstances. Can you sense God's tenderness toward you? He is pouring out His love, even now.

The stories in this book are filled with XOXO moments. May they serve as a reminder of the Lord's ongoing affection toward you. His love never fails, even on the darkest of days. So, lift your heads! Throw wide those arms and prepare yourself for a heavenly embrace as never before. And may you never forget those XOXOs are meant to be shared with those around you.

God's
Greatest
Treasure

This is my wish for you:
comfort on difficult days, smiles when
sadness intrudes, rainbows to follow
the clouds, laughter to kiss your lips,
sunsets to warm your heart,
hugs when spirits sag, beauty for
your eyes to see, friendships to
brighten your being, faith so that
you can believe, confidence for when
you doubt, courage to know yourself,
patience to accept the truth,
love to complete your life.

UNKNOWN

When you think of the word "treasure," what comes to mind? A pirate's treasure chest, overflowing with rubies, diamonds, and other expensive jewels? A lifetime of savings, tucked away in a bank account for retirement or a rainy day? A pocketbook stuffed with cash? The word "treasure" conjures up such images, doesn't it? But could there be more to this word? Something spiritual, perhaps?

The Bible has a lot to say about treasures. We're warned not to give our heart to earthly treasures, and we're also told that the kingdom of heaven is like a treasure hidden in a field. The wise men brought treasures to the baby Jesus as gifts, and we're told that if we sell our possessions and give them to the poor, we will have a treasure in heaven. Yes, those jewelicious images can be found from cover to cover in God's word.

But is there more, perhaps? Have we somehow overlooked the greatest treasure of all—God's love toward us, even when we don't deserve it? Oftentimes this amazing love is poured out in vast, immeasurable ways, nearly overwhelming us. We sense His presence, relish His nearness. We see it as a treasure, available for the taking. The loveliest of all gifts. Other times, we see snatches of His love; just enough to serve as a reminder that He hasn't forgotten us. We can't fully see inside the treasure chest to know what's available to us because we're so distracted with the cares of life.

Oh, if only we could! God has such amazing things in store for us—in good seasons and bad. He longs to teach us a lesson—that we, His children, have great value. In fact, He's already got future blessings in mind for us, even now. He longs to surprise us when we least suspect it. He also longs for us to see the value in others, and to extend love to them even when it seems difficult.

If you're going through a difficult season, don't be discouraged. Instead, trust God. He longs to reach out and touch you with His love as never before. And what a gift that love is! Indeed, it's the greatest treasure of all—greater than all the diamonds and rubies in the world. It shimmers and shines above any other jewel, and its value is immeasurable. Best of all, we didn't have to earn it, and we don't have to wait until we've retired to enjoy it. It was poured out freely on the cross, and is available for the taking. And giving.

As you spend some time reflecting on His marvelous love, be on the lookout for XOXO moments. The Lord might just give you a glimmer of His affection in ways you don't expect. If such a moment comes, see it for what it is—an unparalleled treasure.

*"The kingdom of heaven is like treasure hidden in a field.
When a man found it, he hid it again, and then in his joy
went and sold all he had and bought that field."*

Matthew 13:44 niv

Recycled Treasure

BY KIMM REJD-MATCHETT

There's an old saying that goes, "One man's trash is another man's treasure." My grandfather Charlie took that saying to heart. He saw great purpose in everything— from day-old doughnuts, which the town doughnut store would keep "just for Charlie," to broken glass and rusty nails, to the wounded, broken down people living on the wrong side of the tracks (or in his case, the trailer park across the road).

He would often make trips to the junkyard where he may or may not have been taking trash. Whether or not he left home with something in the back of his little red pickup, we could anticipate that he would eventually return with much more than he left with. Through his beautiful eyes, one of which was prosthetic and completely useless, he saw treasure in every pile of retrieved junk. My dear, sweet, and oh-so-patient grandmother Charlotte would just look out the window and shake her head, never saying a word about the sheds full of grandpa's "treasure" that were spread out along the back of their acreage.

One thing Grandpa Charlie grew especially excited over and would inevitably cause a sparkle to glitter in his one good eye was broken-down bicycles; it seemed like his yard was filled with them. Flat tires, twisted metal, plastic pedals, or ripped bike seats. Anywhere your eye might fall, there were sure to be bits and pieces of broken bicycles.

You see, Grandpa loved to see broken, discarded things come alive. He would get up long before the sun and begin tinkering with the broken pieces of bicycle. He would straighten the bent handles from one and lovingly put it on the unbroken frame of another. Adding patches and blowing up tires, sanding wooden blocks to replace the worn plastic pedals, he would eventually come up with a completely safe, albeit multicolored, usable bicycle. Once complete, he would set the newly revised bicycle over in the bike rack made from recycled, twisted lumber and rusty nails which he would tediously straighten—or get the grandchildren to straighten when they were showing signs of boredom—and smile.

If you paid attention, you would see him watching very closely. He wasn't concerned about the bikes being stolen. He purposely made the bikes for those children across the road who didn't have shoes, let alone bikes. Two or three of those kids would eventually wander into the yard knowing that my grandpa Charlie thought they were absolutely the best kids in the world and go directly to the bike rack. Walking around it and eyeing each recycled bike with precision and nervousness, the children would find one that fit them just perfectly—almost as if it had been made for them—and my grandpa would beam with joy.

My grandfather would then walk out from around the corner and gladly say, "Well I'll be jiggered, that looks perfect for you. I think you should have it!" Then he would help the child climb aboard and ride away. He became known throughout town for such treasures and often someone would drive into his yard with a couple of kids in the back and ask if this was the place where "my kids could get a bike." That would generally open the door for my grandpa to sit and smile and listen as yet another lonely parent would regurgitate a story of bad luck and hard times.

Eventually calling the kids out of the backseat to choose a bike deeply blessed Grandpa, and the parent would feel just a bit relieved as they received a firm handshake, often a bear hug, and the heartfelt words of "you come on back anytime." They usually would.

As time always does, it sped by quickly with Grandpa's eccentric ways remaining constant. The piles of treasure grew bigger and Grandpa grew older. One sad spring day, cancer caught up and grabbed tightly onto Grandpa Charlie. Not long after, we all gathered and heartbreakingly watched as a beautiful brand-new burial casket was lowered ever so gently and swallowed up by the earth.

The family chose to have a gathering the night before his funeral where we could share stories and enjoy memories. The stories told were not of great wealth or who got his boat or vacation spots. He had none of that. No, the stories told were of his outrageous generosity with the little he did have—memories of his oversized heart and genuine love and compassion for everyone alike.

There were tears and sadness, but they were greatly overshadowed by the beaming pride we all carried out of the gathering that night as we realized how greatly we had all been affected by the model Grandpa Charlie had lived out before us.

When eventually we could face the fact that he was gone, nearly all fifty members of Grandpa's family got together for a work bee for the sole purpose of digging through sheds and returning most of his treasure to the junkyard where we all thought it belonged.

We still had failed to see through his eyes and now found it nearly impossible to find even the tiniest bit of value in the heaps of trash he had collected over the years.

Except. . .

The aunts picked up this or that and quietly stashed it into their cars to take home. I also noticed a few uncles pick up a tool or a can of screws that they'd stealthily throw into the back of their pickups hoping nobody was noticing that they, too, were beginning to see treasure amid the trash. I, too, began to see through Grandpa's eyes, and the back of my van soon housed numerous treasures.

Old, weathered barn windows stacked not-so-neatly in one forgotten shed surrounded by broken pieces of wood or buckets of rusty springs. Today, those old weathered barn windows can be found at antique stores or rustic tea shops for a pretty penny, and anyone who is at all interested in antique things loves to get her hands on such an item.

One of my most valued treasures from that day was an old metal bed frame, which I carted home and joyfully used for years. It was fantastically comfortable with the old-style springs and solid as rock because of the steel bars beneath holding it all together. A treasure to be sure!

Grandpa Charlie seemed to have an eye for treasure after all. The family used to enjoy teasing him, vowing to one another never to be like him and swearing we'd disown each other if sadly, one of us did decide to see treasure in trash. We would roll our eyes and emphatically deny that the old man in the little red truck loaded up with junk was our grandfather. Today, we are proud he was.

Grandpa Charlie was quirky and wonderful. He had one eye that saw and one ear that heard. He was missing more fingers than he wasn't. He loved to tease his grandchildren and play cards, cheating and smirking and laughing all the while but always loving. He purposefully and thoughtfully taught us all about Christ's love, about forgiveness, about loving each other, about family.

What he unknowingly taught us was also deeply valuable and life shaping and Christlike. Grandpa Charlie taught us to see through the eyes of God. When others see junk, God sees value. In things, and more importantly, in people. All are made in the glorious image of God, and all are equally valuable to Him. Grandpa taught us—by example—to find that value in people, no matter what. To look for the down-and-outers and simply love them.

Somewhere along the journey of my life and moving from one place to another, my dearly loved bed was lost. Actually, just the steel rods needed to hold the entire bed together were lost making the bed useless. Because no one else saw the treasure that I saw, I was strongly and repetitively encouraged to get rid of it—return it to where it came from, the junkyard.

I'd likely not find the necessary bars ever again, so I gave in and sadly loaded it into the truck.

Many years later I stumbled upon a recycle shop where I could drop off things I no longer needed and take what I wanted.

I started popping in now and then to this wonderful recycle shop just for the fun of it. I began dropping stuff off, determined not to take anything home. After all, it was junk. About the same time, my family was going through a number of hard things, finances being one of them.

Wandering around the recycle shop one warm spring afternoon, my eyes fell upon something—a treasure. I don't recall exactly what it was, but I remember whispering a very teary, "Thanks, Lord." I instantly had an overwhelming sense that God, maker of heaven and earth, the God who directs lightning and commands thunder, had just given me a special, well thought out gift.

I started going frequently in hopes of finding more of God's little gifts, and He certainly was faithful. More important than the small (sometimes not so small) items I picked up, were the wonderful hurting people that I'd find. Often there would be a single mom who had nothing and came in hopes of finding anything useful no matter how well used or worn-out it was.

One lovely family in particular who was there most of the time had recently experienced the excruciating pain of having their son removed from their home. In desperate attempts to override the hurt of missing him, they would come and fill their van with things "for when Jarod comes home." Sadly, he didn't return, but they continued to go to the recycle and pick things up. God's treasures.

I wouldn't always find a treasure, but every now and then—usually when I needed it most—He would surprise me with something or someone that deeply touched my heart. Every time, His little presents would remind me that

He is with me. His eye is ever on me, and He is aware of me. Better yet, He reminded me with these gifts that He knows exactly how to give me that message so that it will sink in and become meaningful to me.

I soon found that when I'd go out for coffee or milk or to pick up one of my children, my vehicle seemed to make turns I had not intended. Like a horse running to the barn, I'd find myself at the recycle. I would silently hope that the Lord had a treasure for me that day, like He had the day before, just so I could feel that exuberant sense of His care and love all over again. Whether He gifted me with a pretty item or a broken person, the feeling was the same—deep supreme value.

Then one day there it was! As I was wandering around looking for a present for my father, my eye fell on what appeared to be a white metal bed frame. I gasped and excused myself from Patty, a wonderful treasure with whom I was chatting. I tried to walk nonchalantly toward the white metal frame, knowing full well I was half-walking, half-running, and looking like a complete idiot. I hoped I would get there before someone else saw this wonderful treasure and beat me to it. Turns out, nobody else was seeing through my eyes. I finally reached the prize. With tears streaming down my face, I stood there in almost unbelief as I ran my fingers so gently over my bed.

God is love and He loves me. . .and that day He went to extra special lengths to make sure I heard Him telling me. Because Patty watched me act so silly over an old scratched metal bed frame, I had to explain the story to her. I told her about my grandpa Charlie. I was able to share with her just how very much God loves us and what lengths He goes to just to show us His love.

I have my dearly loved bed back, and I am so excited each time I look at it or run my fingers along the cracked white paint or curl up in its soft, welcoming comfort. God Himself gave me a gift, knowing exactly how to tune in my ears to hear His voice. I also have a new friend who knows just how valuable God is and how valuable I think *she* is, too.

While God gave me my bed back, He gifted me with a much more valuable treasure that day. He gifted me hope. He gifted me peace. He gifted me the unforgettable message that while I may be unaware of Him, He is always aware of me. He knows what touches my heart and is eager to do just that.

It never ceases to amaze me—the impact people can have on us without even intending to. I am forever grateful for the things my grandfather taught me. I know the Lord intimately because my grandfather genuinely loved the Lord intimately and encouraged me to do the same. I have an ability to see treasure in trash and the value in people because my grandfather chose to see through the eyes of the Father and taught me to do the same.

Thanks, Grandpa.

The Least
of These

What does love look like?
It has the hands to help others.
It has the feet to hasten to the
poor and needy. It has eyes to see
misery and want. It has the ears to
hear the sighs and sorrows of men.
That is what love looks like.

SAINT AUGUSTINE

Sometimes we get so wrapped up in our own lives that we don't take the time to focus on those around us, particularly those in need. If you've ever been through a difficult financial season, perhaps you're more aware of the needs of those who are hurting. You notice them at every turn. God longs for us to reach out and touch people, just as He reaches out and touches us. In fact, He often gives us imaginative and creative ways to do just that. And why not? Hasn't He been creative in the many ways He's reached out to us in our pain? Sure He has. He longs for us to be just as creative as we touch the lives of those around us.

Think about it for a moment. God, the Creator of the universe, could give a starving man a cupboard full of food in the blink of an eye. But most often, He chooses to prick our hearts, encouraging us to give, instead. He could place a blanket in a shivering woman's path, but, instead, niggles at our conscience until we purchase a blanket to give her.

Why does God so desperately want us to reach out to those who are hurting, lonely, and needy? There's a short answer to this question, of course: We're all God's kids, and He loves us. There's a long answer, too: We are all starving beggars in His sight—children who could never survive without a heavenly handout. In other words, we're all in need—internally and externally. And He's the great "Meeter" of needs. So, why use us? The Lord of the universe longs to involve us in the process, not only to teach us some sort of great lesson, but so that He can bless us, as well.

It's a wonderful feeling, to be used of God to meet the needs in other people's lives. We have the opportunity to help them out, sure, but there's more to it than that. God wants to touch something deep inside us. Giving stirs up an extreme gratitude inside the giver. It reminds us that "There but for the grace of God go I." It puts things in perspective.

Giving does something else, too. When we look into the eyes of the recipient, we see Jesus. That's right. Jesus. He's the beggar on the street. He's the single mom who can't pay her rent. He's the hungry child shivering in the corner of the unheated room. And when we reach out and give, help, touch, love, hug. . .we're not just doing it to the person in need, we're doing it to—and for—Jesus.

Who have you touched today? Who do you plan to touch? If you begin to look for ways to bless, you will surely find them. And how exciting to think that your simple act of kindness could be the very heavenly hug that person needs to make it through the day.

"And the King will say, 'I tell you the truth, when you did it to one of the least of these my brothers and sisters, you were doing it to me!'"

MATTHEW 25:40 NLT

The Messenger

By David McLaughlan

My grandmother was the daughter of Irish immigrants. The men of her family lived hard lives working in coal mines or the local iron foundry. As a relief from this poorly paid, back-breaking labor, they made regular use of the local hostelries and yelled away their tensions every Saturday supporting the local football team.

With six surviving children, a husband, and a widowed mother to look after—and very little money to do it with—Granny just got on with life. We kids never thought to wonder where she got her strength from. We would descend on her house every weekend assured of food, love, and freedom.

Many of our favorite childhood memories were gifts from her. They do say that I once paraded up and down the avenue in my diaper wearing her high heels, Sunday bonnet, and pearls! Grandpa was there and he was a good guy, but men of his generation didn't really play with children. Their contribution was working to make sure we were fed and had beds to sleep in. He used to tell us he would leave the house at five in the morning, walk two miles to the south, drop half a mile down a mine shaft, then walk two miles north again to the coal face. He joked he would be quicker sinking a shaft in his vegetable patch.

Twenty years after he died, part of his vegetable patch actually sank into the ground. A steady breeze blew up from that hole until the local council filled it with concrete. But before they did that, I once watched Granny standing by the hole and gazing down. I wondered if she was now breathing the same long-buried air he had breathed all those years before.

Looking back it is obvious she found her strength in faith. Because she was the only one in the family who did, we kids tended to think that was just Granny's way. We never thought any more about it. She went to church every Sunday until her legs couldn't make the walk anymore. Then one of the congregation would take her by car. Then the minister would bring the service to her. We could see all this happen, but none of us got it.

When she finally went to her heavenly home, her grown-up children were distraught. There was no spiritual comfort from them. They just wanted to clear the house as soon as possible and get on. Very few mementos were kept.

Practically everything was put out for the bin men. I guess it was just their way of dealing with the grief. She had been the rock their family was built on.

But on a rainy afternoon, three days later, her teenage grandson went back to her strangely empty house and searched through the trash cans. In the end I came away with only two things—a soggy suitcase of family photos and her Bible.

During the next several years, I made good use of those photos, copying them, printing them off for family events, and showing them to my own children. I used to leaf through the well-thumbed Bible and wonder what she got from it. But I really had no idea. It didn't speak to me.

With Granny gone there was no faith influence in my growing up—and I didn't miss it. I was a rationalist, an intellectual. If there wasn't an explainable answer, then, as far as I was concerned, it was a dumb question.

My wife didn't think so, and I used to tease her it for. It was easy to poke fun at her faith. But then, isn't it always easier to criticize? Thankfully, she loved me more than I annoyed her.

On the train heading for an evening out in the city, I raised a subject I'd read about the day before.

"Is your churchgoing a substitute for Christianity?" Julie looked puzzled, so I explained. "It's about folk who claim to be Christian because they go to church every Sunday but don't actually live their faith in any practical way for the other six days of the week."

Well, we tossed the idea about for a few minutes. Sadly there are enough folk who live like that to make it a fairly easy target to hit. But, as Julie pointed out, faith is such a personal thing it's often hard to tell what it means to different individuals or how it affects their lives.

To be honest, I wasn't really that interested anyway. I was quite certain in my beliefs, and they didn't involve some big guy in robes floating about on a cloud. I wasn't looking for an answer; I was just passing time on a train and scoring some lazy points.

Then the train reached the end of the line. Once in the station we made our way through the masses of travelers toward the exit. You know what it's like; you focus on the people directly in front of you while others flow past on either side. All I was concerned with was getting out onto the street and finding a coffee shop before we went to the theater. The last thing I expected was to have my question put to the test almost immediately.

My wife tugged at my sleeve. "Look." She pointed through the crowd. I saw a bank of pay phones against the far wall. *So what?* I thought. Then I saw what she had seen. A hunched, elderly lady was moving from phone to phone, checking every change return slot.

Looking at her many layers of ragged clothing and shoes held together with silvery duct tape, Julie commented, "She's probably wearing everything she owns.

And what she isn't wearing is probably in the plastic bag she's carrying."

I found a gap in the tide of people and stood for a moment, just watching her. Having found no forgotten change, this woman, who had to be in her eighties, headed for the newspaper shop.

She was so small I doubt the sales assistant ever saw her among the genuine customers. She picked up a magazine or two and "accidentally" shook out the advertising leaflets and free TV guides. She picked these up off the floor and tucked them into one of her many cardigans.

"Why's she doing that?" Julie asked. I could only guess they might be to help her through a cold night. I'd heard that crumpled paper stuffed inside clothes was a good insulator. But I'm sure it isn't anyone's idea of a cozy night. Maybe she rationalized that she wasn't stealing if she only took the stuff the newspapers gave away for free.

By now I was feeling like something of a voyeur. It was time to move on. I had seen poor people before. On the streets of Glasgow that night, I would probably walk past a dozen professional beggars. Life goes on. There was coffee and a show waiting for me.

But I couldn't walk away.

This was what I had been talking about on the train. How many of the folk walking past were churchgoers? But no one stopped to help. *How about you?* my conscience asked. *Are you any better than that?*

Well, I think of myself as a nice guy, but this was something different. There was a powerful urge keeping me there.

Once again the woman made her way, almost invisibly, through the crowd. Her next stop was the photo booth, where she pressed the coin return button a few times.

When she came out, I was standing in front of her. She stopped, but didn't really seem to see me.

"Find anything?" I asked. She jumped in surprise and looked up at me, her face a picture of confusion. She didn't seem to think I was police, or security, or railway staff. She didn't seem afraid. She just seemed totally confused by the fact that someone was paying attention to her.

What must it be like, I wondered, to live a life where being acknowledged is a startling experience?

"Here." I held out some money.

Her face ran through a range of expressions and her mouth moved, but the two seemed disjointed, out of sync. I had the distinct impression she was trying to remember how to speak. She shook her head, smiled, and her lips formed a silent thank-you.

Then it happened.

Stunned and scared, I stepped back into the crowd. By the time I reached my wife again, my tears were flowing freely.

Well, of course I told Julie what had happened, but I didn't tell anyone else. After all, I didn't believe in that kind of thing. To believe the evidence of my eyes meant reevaluating the whole world I lived in.

A few weeks later, I went back to the station to look for that old lady. What I was hoping to prove by finding her I had no idea. It didn't matter; she wasn't there.

I went back the following week with the same results.

By the third week, I was beginning to wonder about myself. What was this obsession all about? Was I actually starting to lose my mind? Why else would I be stalking an anonymous bag lady?

Then I saw her. She was going through the same routine. I watched her check the phone coin slots, shake the inserts out of newspapers, and head for the photo booth. I followed her, not knowing what I was going to say, but hoping the transport police weren't watching me and wondering what I was up to.

I found myself in front of her for the second time, still not knowing what I was going to say. She looked up, curious, quizzical. "How are you doing?" I asked. She replied in a language that wasn't a language. I tried again. "Can I, maybe. . .help you with something?" There were more nonsensical sounds in reply.

And there was nothing there. The thing that had kept me coming back in search of her was nowhere to be seen. She was simply a confused old lady, living a hard life at the end of her days.

I pushed some money into her hand.

"God bless you!" I had never said that to anyone ever before. But my first meeting with this woman had hit my heart hard.

I'd thought it was enough to be a good man and do good things. I was kind of aware that it mattered how I lived my life—but that never squared with my "once you're dead, you're dead" philosophy. After teasing my wife about her faith, I tried to do a "meaningless" good deed and was immediately shown the meaning. I saw why it mattered.

If God, or His Son, had chosen to show himself to me through that old lady, well. . .to be honest, I might not have recognized either of them. So, instead, He sent a messenger, someone I certainly would recognize. For a second or two that deeply lined gray face and those watery blue eyes had been replaced by a fuller face and emerald green eyes. It was a face I hadn't seen for over twenty years. It was the face of someone I still loved with the pure love of a child. My Granny.

And she was smiling. She was happy with me.

The tears are back as I write this, and I know, at last, what sustained her. I also know that her lifelong struggle was the least of her worries.

That old Bible I rescued from the trash sits on my shelf now. It's more worn now than when she used it. It speaks to me now.

Julie and I had been on our way to see *Jesus Christ Superstar* in the theater that night. I'm sure it was a good show, but I confess I only saw about half of it. The rest was blurred by tears of happiness.

Good Gifts

Use what talents you possess;
the woods would be very silent
if no birds sang there except
those that sang best.

HENRY VAN DYKE

Have you ever considered the fact that our talents and abilities are a reflection of God's love and tenderness toward us? He speaks to us through them. If you've been graced with a lovely singing voice, the ability to play an instrument, or other gifts, praise God! All good gifts come from Him. And He often uses those gifts to minister—not just to those around us, but to *us*, as well.

So, what gifts have you been given? Are you a strong academic? Do certain sports come naturally to you? Are you a whiz with numbers? Have you been given the gift of song or dance? Instead of taking these things for granted, instead of saying, "Oh, everyone in my family is musical," consider the fact that the Lord strategically dropped that very gift into your life because He knew He could trust you with it.

Wow! That puts things in perspective, doesn't it? You weren't gifted by accident. That talent or ability was deliberately placed inside you, God's child. So, what are you going to do with this gift He has entrusted to you? Hide it away? Pretend it doesn't exist? Flaunt it to the masses, proclaiming your gift is greater than someone else's? The choice is completely up to you, of course.

God gives us gifts, primarily, so that they can be used for Him. We're instructed to go into all the world and preach the gospel. . .to reach out to others, proclaiming the Good News. Maybe you can't leave the country. Maybe you can't even leave the town you live in. But you can—right where you're planted—use the gifts God has placed inside you to proclaim His goodness to those around you.

Today, begin to think of ways you can reach out to others in your neighborhood, community, or town using your talents and abilities. Get creative. Ask the Lord for divine inspiration. Then take that gift you've been given and fine-tune it, making it the best it can be. Practice, practice, practice. When you're ready, hit the streets running. Find a way to be usable. Always give Him the glory and never take the credit for the gifts you've been given.

And while you're at it, why not stir up the gifts in others? If you're a musician, take a young musician under your wing. If you're a sports enthusiast, begin to train youngsters to play ball. If you're a strong academic, offer to tutor those who are not. In other words, pass on the gift you've been given. In doing so, you'll be sending heavenly hugs to all in your path.

"If you, then, though you are evil, know how to give good gifts to your children, how much more will your Father in heaven give good gifts to those who ask him!"

MATTHEW 7:11 NIV

Imagine

By Charles F. Miller

Have you ever been privileged? I don't mean the everyday sense of, "Thank you a lot, I sure appreciate that, that's terrific" kind of privilege; I mean cosmically, universally, heavenly privileged?

I am a nonmusician from a musical family. At St. John's Episcopal Church in Royal Oak, Michigan, where I grew up, Mom and I would sit separately on the side—because everybody else in the family was up front making music. My brother is a terrific singer who married a terrific singer; my sister was a good singer and terrific organist and pianist, who was once chosen to accompany the Detroit Symphony. Mom and I. . .we couldn't carry a tune with a bucket and two hands! It's not that we didn't love to sing, but we were so bad we would throw the people around us off.

And then there was Dad. Dad had the best bass voice I ever heard, as well as being a mathematical genius.

But I get ahead of myself. Dad was born in 1913. He was a man of his generation. He could be gruff and stern; he didn't seem comfortable around small children, even his own. When we became teenagers, though, we found that he could also be very personable and even fun. But raising kids was the mother's job. He was a good father and worked very hard to provide. He was an accountant and an engineer. In World War II he was stationed at Pearl Harbor. He sometimes worked with the code breakers there on the secret Japanese war codes: the infamous "Code Purple." I'm sure that his mathematical skills proved very useful to those guys.

When I was in high school, Dad tried to help me with my algebra. But Dad and I are opposite. Physically, we're almost identical: 5 feet 11 inches, 165 pounds. Our brains, however, are exact opposites. I'm a poet; he was a math whiz. When he tried to help me with the algebra, it quickly became clear to me that while I was trying to figure formulas and rules on the paper, Dad was seeing the numbers. They were doing kind of a square dance in his mind—or, rather in his imagination—moving into place almost as soon as he saw them. He couldn't help me. Our minds worked too differently.

Dad suffered from severe Alzheimer's the last nine or ten years of his life. For his last five years, the Alzheimer's was severe enough that he had to stay in a nursing home. But right up to the end, bits of him would shine through, including his mathematical acumen. He was still in the Detroit area; I live in Toledo. I visited him almost every weekend. One Saturday, when his Alzheimer's was quite advanced, I was wheeling him into the dining room. The Muzak radio station was playing from the ceiling. Suddenly, Dad blurted out a number, something like, "$446.34." I remembered the number and wrote it down. It was obviously the price of something. I asked him what he meant, and he, of course, couldn't answer. He didn't remember what he had just done. So I tried to remember what had just come over the radio. I vaguely remembered some sort of financial advertisement, with a popular local DJ as the voice. I figured that maybe the voice had given a price of something at, say, twenty percent off, and Dad had figured out the actual price. That would be like Dad.

So as I stayed with Dad through the afternoon, I listened for that ad again. It turned out to be an ad for a bank's home loan program. It gave a sample loan, something like "a fifteen-year loan for a $120,000 home is just 6.49 percent!" I wrote that down, too. I had to wait until I got home to test my theory about what Dad had done. I had a calculator with financial functions, and when I typed in the numbers my hunch proved correct, if barely believable.

In the space of about ten seconds, Dad—who didn't

know exactly who I was, what year it was, or his own age—had figured out the monthly payment on that sample loan *correct to within a nickel*!

To this day I shake my head when I remember it.

I would take Dad out in his wheelchair during good weather, and we would watch the cars driving along Twelve Mile Road, talk a little, and enjoy getting out. He could name some of the older cars. This was especially fun if there happened to be an antique car show going on somewhere near, and the old cars would drive by, or be taken by on trailers. The older the car, the more likely he could name it.

I discovered that next door to that nursing home is St. David's Episcopal Church. Dad was a lifelong Episcopalian; he became a deacon after he retired. One weekend I had the idea of taking him to St. David's for a service, thinking it would revive memories, thinking that he would probably remember the prayers and some of the hymns, all of which had been very important to him. He had always loved the Episcopal service. I called ahead to see if they could accommodate him. To my surprise, the deacon at St. David's was one of Dad's best friends. They had been right next door to each other for the last couple of years and hadn't realized it. The man was a few years younger than Dad, who was eighty-seven at the time. He and Dad had been friends in the same neighborhood, had gone to the same schools.

They had both been on Oahu during World War II. Dad was in the navy; his friend in the army. They played golf together there, their units played baseball games against each other, and they had swum together at Waikiki. . .after the navy finally decided that there was no further threat of Japanese invasion, and it was okay to take the rolls of barbed wire off the beach! This friend, an army officer, had even sneaked Dad—a navy enlisted man—into the army officers' club a few times. A rare treat.

I remembered this man and his wife as good friends of my parents, after the war, back when I was a kid. And when Dad and I finally went to the church on a Sunday morning, Dad immediately smiled, laughed, and called his friend and his wife by their first names! It was the only time he would remember anyone's first name without prompting, during the last five or six years of his life. I got goose bumps—and not for the last time.

As I've said, Dad had the best bass singing voice I ever heard, live or recorded. Those who had heard him earlier in his life agreed. And I mean *bass*. . .sub-basement bass. "Yes, he can hit *that* note" bass: resonant, clear, precise, and incredibly powerful at the same time. In all the singing that Dad did, I can never remember him using a microphone, and he sang in some pretty big places. St. John's was a cathedral-style church—the ceiling was three floors up there. But he never used a microphone. He could, however, also bring a song down to a whisper, and bring you to tears. While he was still in high school in Royal Oak, he had started singing the lead in local productions of light operas: Rogers and Hammerstein, and the others of that time. He worked his way through two years at the University of Denver by singing lead for the Denver Opera Company.

When I was young, we would go to a couple of Detroit Tigers games a year. We always sat along the first base line, and I'm sure, in the cozy little bandbox of Tiger Stadium, that his voice could be clearly heard by the folks sitting behind third base. For a while it kind of made me cringe. After I'd grown up a little, I stood tall and wanted to tell everybody: "You hear that voice? That's my dad!"

I've often thought that part of the grumpiness that Dad sometimes showed was because of frustration that he hadn't found a way to make a living with his voice, and with the acting that went along with it. I don't know if he even tried. It's just a theory. He certainly worked at his skill like a professional.

By the time he was eighty, when Alzheimer's started to show itself, Dad's voice was a shadow of what it had been, though you could still hear echoes of it at Christmastime or at church. He was never, however, off-key. As the Alzheimer's developed, his voice seemed to disappear. One of the problems he developed was an extreme difficulty swallowing. I figured that this had also put an end to his singing. The only thing he seemed to want to do with music anymore was listen to it.

So I didn't know quite what to expect when we went to St. David's. He surprised me a little by singing the hymns, or attempting to. He couldn't quite keep up with the rest of the congregation. He'd get the first part of the line out pretty well, but then he'd fall behind. He remembered the prayers of the service, too, but it was the same thing. He remembered them, or most of them, but he couldn't speak fast enough to keep up.

St. David's had an organist who was fairly well-known in classical music circles, judging from what he played at the beginning of the service, and from what the bulletin said about his concerts. So I wasn't surprised when he started playing an extended piece after the service was over.

It was not a fancy organ piece. It sounded like variations on a hymn, though I didn't recognize the tune. It had the regular rhythm and melody of a hymn, and soon Dad was humming along—in harmony, of course. Then he switched from humming, to kind of singing along by just going "Aaahhh-aah-aah-aaahhh. . ." When he did that, it sounded to me as if he had suddenly gone horribly off-key. My immediate thought was, *I guess Dad's finally lost it*. Then he'd go back to humming, and get back on-key. He'd do the hum for fifteen or twenty seconds, then the "Aaahhh. . ." for fifteen or twenty seconds.

Then I leaned over a little closer, because I couldn't really believe that those awful sounds were coming out of my dad. I listened more carefully. When he switched from humming to the "Aaaah-aah-aaaaah" singing, he was actually switching to the most exquisite, intricate, minor-key accompaniment imaginable, weaving it almost like a violin part around the major-key organ solo; almost like a bass equivalent to a soprano's "descant." It was as if he were taking the straight thread of the organ's melody, and braiding, spiraling a minor key color around it like a helix of DNA, like the tracings of a ballet. It was mesmerizing. I have never heard anything like it, before or since. Suddenly, I was somewhere else.

Deep down inside my father, the musician was very much alive, maybe better than ever. Dad was in a place where he could be perfectly relaxed, with old friends, where he could be totally unselfconscious. Earlier, I had been given a glimpse through the fog of Alzheimer's into what his mind could do with numbers. Now, while he was listening to music as he had always loved it, I was being given a glimpse through the unselfconsciousness of Alzheimer's into music as Dad had always *imagined* it.

This lasted for six or seven minutes, until the organ solo was finished. And I was the only one who could hear it. I got goose bumps. When it was done, I began quietly weeping at the pure privilege of being the one in the family who was honored to hear this. For a while, I couldn't bring myself to get up, grab the handles of Dad's wheelchair, and take him back. *If there is a heaven, this must be what music is like there,* I thought.

But do you know what the best part is? When I describe this for people who knew Dad's love for music, people who heard him sing. . .

. . .*they believe me.*

Spin It
His Way

If you don't like something,
change it; if you can't change it,
change the way you think about it.

MARY ENGELBREIT

Because we're individuals, we all put our own unique spin on things. We view things differently. We tend to run life's circumstances and situations through our own personal filter, which colors them a certain way. My filter is different from yours, and yours is different from the next guy's.

Consider this scenario: A car accident takes place in the middle of a busy intersection. Ten people could all witness the same accident, and each would have his unique perception (or view) of what had taken place. I might spin the story one way—focusing on the people in the vehicles. You might spin it another—focusing on the damage to the cars. Another bystander might focus his version of the story on the condition of the dog in the road—the cause of the accident in the first place. The police officer's spin, no doubt, would be on settling the issue of who was at fault. The insurance adjuster would have his own spin, too. Likely, he would spin the story to make sure the insurance company didn't have to pay more than necessary.

Yes, perceptions are definitely unique to the individual. And because they are, they can be tricky at times. Sometimes we over-spin things, making mountains out of molehills. False perceptions can cause us to get discouraged when there's really no need for discouragement. On the other hand, godly perceptions can lift our spirits, even when everything around us seems hopeless. It's all in how we spin it. A financial bump in the road might send one person into a panic, but only cause a little hiccup for another. A medical problem might seem like the end of the road to one, but a chance to trust God for another.

So how do you spin life's difficulties? Do you have a "woe is me" attitude, or do you try to give things a positive spin? Oh, what a joy to stumble across a person whose perceptions come into alignment with God's. People like this have a great disposition, don't they? And why not? The Bible instructs us to have the mind of Christ. We're told in Philippians 2:5 that our attitude should become like that of Jesus. It's time to spin things His way!

Impossible, you say? Not so! We just have to ask for His vision, His attitude, His view of life. We have to renew our minds. Sure, circumstances might be bad, but our thinking doesn't have to be. We can get rid of that stinkin' thinkin' and replace it with a Christlike viewpoint. When we see things through His eyes, everything looks right again.

So, how's your perception today? If you're struggling in this area, it's time to visit the ultimate spin doctor. He'll put everything into alignment.

In your relationships with one another,
have the same mindset as Christ Jesus.

PHILIPPIANS 2:5 NIV

The Brick Baby

By David McLaughlan

It was just a throwaway comment—if you believe in such things—but it led me to one of those moments that will warm my heart in my old age.

I was interviewing someone about a Spitfire aircraft that had crashed in a Scottish loch during World War II. The man I was talking to had been part of the team that recovered the wreck fifty years after it went down. He had lived in the area a long time. "If you want a good story," he said, "you should try and find some oot-by hurds. Their way of life is almost gone from memory now."

Oot-by hurds? I was curious, if confused.

"Hurds," he explained, were shepherds. "Oot-by" referred to the fact that they lived "oot" in the hills with their flocks, as opposed to the more civilized kind who lived "in-by" around the farms.

I had visited some of the tumbledown cottages in the middle of nowhere while hill-walking and had always wondered at the lives of the people who built them and the generations who lived in them. So I got in touch with a newspaper in the Scottish Borders area. They published my request and my phone number. It turned out the first folk to respond didn't live too far from me.

Sorn is a pretty village. You don't pass through it to get to anywhere; you have to actually seek it out. A few streets, a shop that also serves as a post office, a play park, and the remains of a castle on the hill. That's where Jimmy and Morag lived.

They were both in their eighties. Jimmy was a shepherd, the fifth generation of "hurds" in his family. Morag was the daughter of a shepherd and the wife of a shepherd. It had apparently been love at first sight when Jimmy's family had moved to a neighboring farm. He was fourteen; she was twelve. Neither of them ever looked that way at anyone else. Seventy-some years later, they were obviously still as much in love as ever.

They invited me into their home like I was family.

"Doesn't he remind you of. . . ?" Morag said, with a finger to her mouth.

"He certainly does." Jimmy answered her unfinished question.

"You look very like our boy," Morag explained. "He carries a bit extra weight as well."

Had I just been insulted? But something about this charming couple suggested they had never insulted anyone in their lives. Somehow their simple honesty completely disarmed me. I settled in like I was family.

All around the sunlit room were paintings and statuettes of border collie sheepdogs. When I asked if he ever got sentimentally attached to any of his dogs, Jimmy dismissed them as tools of the trade—but it was obvious that many of them had found warm places in his heart.

In one corner of the room stood several shepherds' crooks with the ornate, curving heads he had carved from discarded ram's horns.

We chatted the afternoon away, and Jimmy gave me more than enough information and anecdotes to fill the article I was planning to write. My favorite was when he talked about spending the night on the hills with pregnant ewes who were having difficulty lambing.

Now, even in springtime, the Scottish hills can still be snowcapped. In the middle of the night, with no shelter, they would have been bitter places to hang around.

Jimmy described how he would pull his collar up and pull his hat down. Then he would "hunker doon" beside the ewe. That way he would right on hand if the ewe needed help.

"Must've been lonely at times, though," I suggested.

"Acht." He waved a dismissive hand. "It's a poor sort of fellow who can't put up with his own thoughts for a night.

And when I got fed up talking to myself, I would listen to the Lord talk."

All the while Morag hovered near the side of her husband's high-backed chair. She would be adding to his stories, prompting memories, and going back and forth to the kitchen for tea, biscuits, or whatever else she could offer her guest.

I thanked them for a delightful afternoon and said I'd be in touch when the article was published. I got the feeling they were sad to see me go. Morag escorted me to the door. Jimmy wasn't too good on his feet.

Walking down the hall, her mothering instinct wouldn't let me leave without first asking if I wanted something to eat or drink for the trip home. Did I need to visit the toilet before I left?

I assured her I would be fine and said I had to pick up my daughter from school. I ventured that life for a modern six-year-old would be very different from Morag's childhood on the hills.

Now it was her turn to reminisce.

School had been fun. Of course it was a seven-mile walk to get there. There were maybe a dozen children in the whole school, and their homes were scattered all over the county.

Morag's home was so isolated her mother had once been cut off by snow for eight weeks while her father took the flock farther south. She just got on with raising her children and nursing her baby. There was nothing else for it, and it's what Morag's father would have expected her to do.

It used to be one of Morag's many chores to sweep the snow from the stream that ran past the front door, crack the ice, and bring in the water for the day.

Shopping was done once a month, and Morag used to look for her father coming back over the crest of the hill with the farmer's borrowed horse. He would be perched on the horse's rump, because the saddle would be laden with sacks of flour and the like.

The flour sacks, once emptied, would be bleached and filled with goose feathers to make pillows for the bed. Sometimes, if they had plenty of pillows, the sack would be made into underwear!

Living in the hills meant Morag didn't have many friends, but every once in a while her father would bring a sickly lamb in for her to nurse. There was one in particular she called Rosie. Morag would cuddle her and feed her from a milk bottle with a rubber teat. After Rosie was strong enough to rejoin the flock, Morag would shout her name as she walked past. A woolly head would always rise up from the crowd and reply, "Mehhhhhhhh."

"What about toys?" I asked.

"Oh, there was no money for toys."

Back then Morag's father was paid fifty pounds a year—and a pig! So luxuries like toys were scarce.

"How did you celebrate Christmas out there in the hills?"
I asked.

"With prayers and hymns," Morag replied, and her smile
brought a lump to my throat.

Different branches of the family would tramp across
the hills to gather in one cottage. Usually they would go
to the house that had the youngest children. After all, a
midwinter hike through snow could be tough on young
legs or a mother carrying a child. Then, by lamplight, they
reminisced, caught up, and praised the Lord.

The pig her father had been fattening all year would be
butchered, and several families would be well fed over the
Christmas and New Year period.

"It wasn't really about gifts," she went on, "it was
about God and family. We might be given a sugar mouse
and a piece of fruit. But, ohhh, one year I got hold of a
catalog. There was a baby doll in there, and I wanted
it so much. I was only six, after all! Well, of course,
father and mother didn't have any money for such
things. So father made me a pram from an apple box
and some wheels, and mother wrapped a brick up in a
baby blanket."

A brick? I wondered if she was kidding. I couldn't imagine any child these days being pleased with a brick for a gift.
But Morag's gaze seemed to have left the here and now as
she thought back across the years.

"Oh, I loved my brick baby so much, and I was as proud as could be pushing it up and down the road in my new pram."

Well, that story stayed with me. How could it not? I wrote it up and sent it to a Sunday newspaper. Not knowing if it had much chance of being published, I didn't think to tell Jimmy and Morag about it.

It did get published. But I missed it. The first I knew about it was when Morag phoned me a few days later. It seemed Jimmy had been taken to the hospital. It wasn't a serious problem but, because of his age, it meant an over-night stay for observation.

Morag had been at a loss. She'd been worried for her hus-band and couldn't remember the last night she had spent without him by her side.

Reluctant to go to an empty bed, Morag sat by the side of her coal fire with the newspaper, hoping it would distract her from the lonely ache she felt. She was surprised to find the story of her long-ago Christmas in print, but as she read it the tale of her brick baby brought back the love and security of her childhood days. Her worries were replaced for a while by warmer, happier thoughts.

She slept soundly that night.

In fact she slept so soundly that she slept in. Rushing to get ready to go and visit Jimmy, she grabbed a handful of flowers from their garden to take with her.

"Oh, I was so embarrassed," she told me on the phone.

"Imagine taking a sick man nothing better than a bunch of his own flowers as a gift."

But Jimmy had dismissed her bedside protestations. The flowers had done for him what the story of the brick baby did for Morag. Those crocuses with their stems wrapped in aluminum foil reminded him of home, a place where he belonged and where he was undoubtedly loved.

Well, Jimmy made it safely back home, and Morag got to fuss over him for a long time.

We kept in touch, and Morag kept me up-to-date with all the family news. She thanked me yet again for giving Jimmy someone else to tell his stories to. The magazine article did make it into print, and they both became local celebrities for a while. It was an honor to be able to do that for them.

All things pass. The days of the oot-by hurds are probably gone. Back then, Jimmy could give medicine to ninety sheep out of a hundred and come back the next day and pick out the remaining ten just by looking at them. These days, sheep are herded by men on four-wheelers and are electronically tagged. But the days of love look are set to last a while longer.

Like most parents, Morag's mother and father did their best for their children but their time was limited and their gifts perishable. No doubt the brick baby was laid aside and forgotten as Morag grew up and met Jimmy. But the love that took a brick and made it a cherished gift for a little girl proved much more durable than earthly things.

I doubt if her mother and father could ever have imagined their humble Christmas present would help their little daughter through a lonely night in her old age some eight decades later.

Since I first wrote this, Jimmy and Morag, the shepherd and the shepherd's wife, have gone to meet the Great Shepherd. But the memory of the brick baby and the love that warmed Morag's heart to the end of her days lives on, with me—and hopefully, with you.

The
Boomerang
Effect

The Christian faith is meant
to be lived moment by moment.
It isn't some broad, general outline—
it's a long walk with a real Person.
Details count: passing thoughts,
small sacrifices, a few encouraging
words, little acts of kindness,
brief victories over nagging sins.

JONI EARECKSON TADA

When you hear the word "reciprocate," what comes to mind? Maybe a friend treats you to lunch this week, so you return the favor and pick up the check next time. Perhaps an acquaintance gives you a Christmas gift, and you feel compelled to purchase one for her, as well. Maybe someone reaches out a hand to you when times are tough, so you pay it forward when you see someone else in need. To reciprocate means to return the favor. To give back. Reciprocating feels mighty good. It gives us that warm, fuzzy feeling inside.

Have you ever considered the fact that God's idea of giving—whether financially or otherwise—is reciprocal? It has a boomerang effect. The details of this plan can be found in Luke 6:38: "Give and it will be given to you." The verse goes on to say that when we give, we will receive. . . not just a little, but more than enough. Of course, we don't give to get. That's not the point. But by the same token, it's impossible to give without getting. What an interesting plan!

It all comes down to motivation. We give with clean hands and pure hearts, out of simple obedience. And when our giving is reciprocated—the boss gives us an unexpected raise, someone picks up the tab for our meal, or we find a twenty-dollar bill in our coat pocket—we see it for what it is, and we're grateful. We recognize God's "boomerang" plan and can sense Him smiling down on the situation.

Lest you think this reciprocal thing is all about finances, be assured. . .it's not! Love is reciprocal, too. When you give it, you always receive it in return. Try it out and see for yourself! When you reach out to others—giving them XOXO moments—you receive unexpected blessings in turn. This isn't a new concept, of course. We learned as children that we should "do unto others" as we would have them do unto us. It's God's plan for happy living!

So how do you plan to give today? Financially? A kind word? A kiss on the cheek? A warm handshake? A meal to a homeless man on the corner? A contribution to a local homeless shelter? Preparing a meal for a homebound elderly person? Whatever you plan to do, do it as unto the Lord, and you can be sure it will come back around to meet you. . .probably when you least expect it! So, go forth. . .and give!

*"Give, and it will be given to you. They will pour into
your lap a good measure—pressed down, shaken together,
and running over. For by your standard of measure
it will be measured to you in return."*

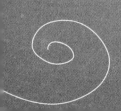

Used Wisely

By David McLaughlan

The theater crowd had just spilled out onto the street. For the past two hours, we had been sitting in plush seats, being wonderfully entertained. Now the still, evening air was full of chatter about the show and what an amazing time everyone had just had. Julie and I were in the middle of it, going with the flow, heading toward the station and the train home.

Then she nudged me and pointed to the edge of the wide sidewalk.

At first I thought he was staff from one of the nearby bars or restaurants putting trash in the Dumpster. He had long, curly, dark hair with flecks of gray through it. Gold-rimmed spectacles rested on his nose. He reminded me of nothing more than the stereotype of a Hebrew scholar. But he wasn't putting stuff in the Dumpster. He was obviously in search of something.

Julie edged me closer.

"Hey," I said as casually as I could. "How you doing there?"

"Just doin' what I need to do to get by," he muttered. He pulled out a french loaf, stuck it in a carrier bag, and went looking for more.

I stood there for a moment, at a loss for what to say next. He steadfastly ignored me and carried on searching. Being watched by me was probably one of the lesser indignities this guy had suffered recently.

"Must be tough," I suggested a little lamely.

I had already spent more than I should have on this lovely night out with my wife. We were only there because the theater was doing a buy-one-get-one-free deal. By most standards I was broke—but then, I wasn't getting my food from a Dumpster.

I had a twenty-pound note in my pocket, about thirty American dollars. I didn't have anything else, so if I was going to help it was that or nothing. My wife, bless her, had already known what I would do when she steered me that way. She also knew we didn't have money to give away, but she wasn't concerned. She's been walking the walk of faith awhile longer than me.

He looked at me for a moment to see if I was serious. "Yeah," he eventually conceded. "Yeah, it is."

"Maybe I can help you a little with that," I said. I held the folded note tucked into my palm as if I was about to shake his hand rather than give him a handout. He knew what I was doing but didn't respond straight away.

"Are you sure?" he asked.

Strangely, I was sure.

He took the money. Then he looked squarely at me. He didn't say thank you. Instead he said, "I'll use it wisely."

I knew what he was telling me. He was reassuring me he wouldn't blow it on drink or drugs. It's probably the main reason a lot of people don't give money to street beggars, the thought that it might be poured down their necks or injected into their veins. This guy hadn't been begging.

I guessed that someone who *would* spend it on drink or drugs might still say the same thing. But. . .

Awhile before that I'd been in a similar position.

No, not searching in a Dumpster or living on the streets. I'd been sitting at home on my nice comfy couch, Web-surfing with the laptop on my knee. Then a message arrived that put a completely different complexion on my morning.

A friend I've known for some time, someone I know to have a kind heart, told me about a foreign student at her college. This girl had been removed from an abusive family situation by the police and was now in a "safe house." So she was in a strange country, hiding from relatives who beat her, unable to give out her address to any potential friends, and trying to get an education on top of all that.

This girl, perhaps wisely, kept to herself. My friend wanted to help but didn't know how. She assured my friend she was eating but, in stark contrast to that claim, she was getting visibly thinner by the day.

Not having much money herself, my friend had taken to practically forcing sandwiches on this reluctant, but still grateful, girl.

It was none of my business, really. It was hundreds of miles away. Surely the college had contingency funds to help out with situations like that. Oh, I had every excuse in the world not to get involved. But if it had been one of my daughters, would I want other people to hide behind excuses—or help? Besides, this had been put in my way now. Was I going to take up the challenge, or was I going to walk on by?

I checked my meager bank account and withdrew 20 percent of all the money I had. I put it in a pretty card, wrote "A gift of love from God" on the inside, and sealed it. I put that in a bigger envelope with my friend's address on the outside. Then I e-mailed her to warn her what was coming. I asked her to pass it on without giving any clue as to where it had come from.

The mailbox is about a three-minute walk from my house. By the time I had posted the card and walked back, the postman had delivered an envelope to my home. In it was a check I didn't remember being owed—for the same amount I had just sent away!

It's nice to think of such things as divine providence, but in reality I didn't want to be taking money from some earthly organization under false pretences. My reputation and any future business I might do with those people could have been at stake.

I phoned the company that sent it. I was sure they didn't owe me any money. They insisted they did. They couldn't provide any details, but they were certain the payment was mine. So who was I to argue?

My card was still sitting in the post box. The student who'd been having such a difficult time was still a day or two away from receiving her gift of love. Even so, I had already been thanked! If I had been there as a fly on the wall to see her open that envelope, I couldn't have been more pleased. I'd done a good thing in God's name and been rewarded.

Or had I? Coincidences happen. This could have simply been an amazing example of one. Well, it would have been— if that was the only time anything like that had happened.

A few months later, and I was poor again. (Can you spot a running theme here?) The bills were getting seriously scary. Lack of money was literally keeping me awake at night. Then a big check arrived for some work I had actually done. Great! I started thinking about which bills to pay first.

Say "Thank You."

It was just a little voice. I ignored it and turned back to the practicalities. I don't like paying bills usually, but getting these taken care of was going to be a real weight off my mind. But that little voice wouldn't go away. It wasn't loud; it just wasn't going to be ignored.

Say, "Thank You," eh?

I remember reading a quote by the monk Meister Eckhart, who said, "If the only prayer you ever pray is, 'Thank You,' it will be enough." Since then, appreciation had been a big part of my prayers.

So I fired up the laptop and electronically zapped some money to a couple of ladies I know who work with orphans and abandoned children in Romania.

This organization, run by a young Californian woman named Sarah and a young German lady named Steffi, does superb work in a hospital in Brasov and out amongst the Roma (gypsy) communities that live on the fringes of Romanian society.

My daughter had volunteered with them for six months, a few years previously. She'd been hugely impressed by the work they did, and I'd kept in touch ever since then. They are in constant need of diaper money, food money, building money, and so on.

Sarah had recently posted a picture on Facebook of a house they built for a Roma family of seven. The walls were rough planks of wood. It was one room with a sloping roof. It stood on four rocks to keep it from soaking up the damp. It was about ten foot by ten foot. In the winter it would all but be buried by the Romanian snow. But the family was delighted to have it. It was a big step up from where they had been living before.

I knew they were all volunteers, and I didn't hesitate to help when I could. If I was looking for a way to express my gratitude with a little money, I couldn't think of any better place to send it—or people more desperately in need of it.

The next morning I got an e-mail from Sarah. She explained she'd been in a meeting about a poor Roma family that needed sponsorship. The woman had been abandoned by her husband. She had eight children and no one to help feed them. Romania isn't big on social security for gypsies. Her extended family already existed below the poverty line. There was no one else to help her.

Sarah was pretty sure she could find them a sponsor, but it might take two months to set up. They needed money to tide this family over until the sponsorship kicked in, and their resources were already stretched.

They simply wouldn't turn the woman and her children away, so they did what they do time and again. Everyone at the meeting offered up a prayer.

How much money did they need to feed a family of nine for two months in Romania? Exactly the amount I had sent. When had this meeting taken place and that prayer been sent up? At the same time as I'd been getting urged to say *thank You.*

How does that happen? Well, as Sarah said, "God knows what He's doing."

And He's not stingy about it, either. The next morning another check arrived in the mailbox. Once again it came from a source I didn't think owed me any money. How much? Three times my thank-you!

Back at the Dumpster I thought of all the ways this guy might use the cash I'd just given him. Drink and drugs were the obvious options, but he didn't look the type. He was relatively clean and still had some self-respect about him. Maybe it would get him a bed for the night, or food he didn't have to mine from a trash pile. Perhaps he had other plans. Maybe he *would* use it wisely.

In the end it didn't matter. I wasn't called to decide how he spent my gift. I was only called to give. After all, I'd had no control over that bank note before it came to be in my pocket. Why would I think I could control it after it left my possession? What this fellow did with it next was between him and God.

I'd be broke for a while, but I was well used to that. I still got by. I still ate. I had already experienced God's providence in similar times, and I already knew that if you give, you *shall* receive.

He'd told me he would use it wisely. I patted him on the shoulder. "Use it how you like, mate," I said. Then Julie and I went on our way.

The one thing I knew for sure about that twenty-pound note was that in giving it away when I needed it, *I* was the one using it wisely!

The God of "Suddenlys"

Miracles are a retelling in
small letters of the very same
story which is written across
the whole world in letters too
large for some of us to see.

C.S. LEWIS

Sometimes God speaks to us in simple, quiet ways—a whisper, a word, or a thought. He gives us heavenly hugs that no one else can see or feel. Other times He intervenes in loud and boisterous ways that stun and mesmerize us. People nearby stand in awe, amazed at what God has done.

Whether we hear His words shouted or whispered, He's always on the move. And you can be assured of one thing: He's still in the miracle-working business today. Don't let the naysayers convince you otherwise. He longs for us to continually anticipate His inevitable, supernatural intervention in our lives. He's going to come through for us. No doubt about it.

Oftentimes we go through difficult seasons and cry out to God, but He doesn't appear to respond, at least not in the way we expect. The silence terrifies us. We need Him to intervene, but it doesn't seem like He's going to. Fear kicks in, and we begin to doubt. More time passes, and we reach the point where we're about to give up. Oh, but that's usually the very moment when the Lord is preparing to move! Many times He waits until the eleventh hour, and then miraculously surprises us—often going above and beyond what we need. Hang on, child! The miracle is on its way!

We learn, through trial and error, that God is in the "suddenly" business. Months go by, and then. . .suddenly! Suddenly, a promotion at work. Suddenly, a healing we've been praying for. Suddenly, a kind word from someone who never treated us well. Suddenly, an unexpected romance. Suddenly, a restored relationship with an absent parent. Suddenly, an opportunity to do something we've always longed to do.

The only problem with "suddenlys" is that we don't know when they're going to take place. Maybe a year will go by, and then "suddenly" God will move. Maybe five years, even. Or ten. So what happens between the point of need and the "suddenly" answer? How do we fill in that gap? With faith, of course.

What sort of miracle do you need today? Do you need physical healing? A financial miracle? Do you need God to sweep in and restore a broken relationship? Instead of focusing on the problem, prepare yourself for God's inevitable supernatural intervention. He's going to come through for you suddenly, when you least expect it. In the meantime, continue to praise Him. That way, when the answer comes, you won't be caught off guard. You'll already have a song of thankfulness on the tip of your tongue.

And my God will liberally supply (fill to the full) your every need according to His riches in glory in Christ Jesus.

PHILIPPIANS 4:19 AMP

Big or Small,
He Can Handle It All

By Angela Deal

A heavy cloud hung over the church. The Barnett family's malicious rumors were spreading, creating a ripple effect of confusion and broken relationships. My husband and I were caught in the cross fire because the Barnetts were our landlords. We were struggling financially, desperate for the acreage they rented to us, because it enabled us to park our thirty-year-old mobile home there while paying off debts. We simply couldn't afford to jeopardize our living arrangements.

But one day, when Mrs. Barnett had pushed too far, Romans 8:31 (NIV) came to mind. *"If God is for us, who can be against us?"*

With a heavy sigh, I finally looked Mrs. Barnett straight in the eyes.

"No," I told her. "We don't agree with you." Then, after explaining my concerns, I said, "Look, Mrs. Barnett, I hope this doesn't destroy our friendship. But friends don't flatter. They speak the truth in love."

"How dare you!" Mrs. Barnett shrieked. "You're not a real friend." After spitting out several more livid words, she yelled, "We want you off our land!" Then she stormed off.

"Oh, God," I prayed, "what have I done? Please help!"

Suddenly, a gentle peace washed over me. *I will not leave you or forsake you*, God whispered.

With God's promises close to our hearts, my husband and I began searching for new living arrangements. But things didn't go so well. First, we hunted for a new location to park our mobile home on. But nothing was available. Either our mobile home was too old to put onto existing town lots or there were no other acreages available in the countryside. Then, when we tried getting a mortgage for a small house, rejection stared us in the face at every turn. Finally, when we searched for a house to rent, nothing was available in our price range. Before long, several weeks had flown by with no sign of help from God.

During that time, we decided to sell an old wooden grain shed that we had fixed up into a one-room cabin, along with a garden shed, a wood shed, a cattle shed, and some fence panels. We were hoping to bring in some extra money for our move, but, so far, we'd only received one response to our advertisements from a lady named Suzy.

"I'm very interested," Suzy said. "I just need to think about it. But, in the meantime, would you call me if anyone else shows interest in it?"

Since Suzy had been the only one to show interest, and since I cleaned the office building where she was employed, I gave her my word.

"Yes," I promised. "I can do that."

Several days passed, but she never called.

My prayers turned from, "Thank You, God. I know You're helping us," to "God, where are You?" *Were all my prayers landing on deaf ears?* I panicked.

I found myself slipping into a dark hole of discouragement as waves of fear washed over me. Had God abandoned us?

I wonder which street corner we should live on? I'd mumble in self-pity.

I knew my simmering hostility toward our circumstances was destructive, but I couldn't shake my feelings.

Finally, I drove over to a friend's house.

"Carol," I said. "I'm sinking fast, and I really need your help."

After explaining our dilemma, Carol smiled and said, "You know, it doesn't matter how big or small our problems are. God is in the business of doing miracles, and He can handle anything."

"Yeah, I know. But I've had serious doubts about that recently, and I've even told God so."

"Well, then, why don't we pray?" Carol suggested.

And, so, we did.

"God," I prayed, "I'm sorry for my rotten attitude and for losing faith in You. Please help me to trust You again."

When I finished, Carol took over.

"Lord," she prayed, "please encourage Angela today. Show her that You are still in control and that You haven't forgotten about her. Please do a miracle for her family."

Fireworks did not explode. We'd just reached out to God in simple prayer, so when I climbed into my car to leave, I never imagined the lengths God might go in answering our prayers. Though discouragement still loomed heavy over me, I felt better because I'd sought and found God's forgiveness for my sour attitude. And that really helped.

As soon as I arrived home, I hit the PLAY button on my telephone answering machine. There was one message.

"Hey, my name is Victor," the message played. "I'm interested in your cabin. Please call me."

"Wow!" I gasped. "This is good news."

Immediately, I phoned Suzy but only got her answering machine.

"Suzy," I said into the recording. "There's someone else interested in the cabin, so I need to know if you're still interested or if I should proceed with this guy? Please call me right away."

I hung up. Then I phoned Victor and explained my circumstances to him.

"Hey, that's not fair!" He griped. "You should sell it to the first person who pays you."

"You're probably right," I said, "but I need to honor my word with her. After all, I clean the office building where she works, so I don't want to create waves with my job."

"Oh, all right," he mumbled. "But can I still look at it in the meantime?"

"Certainly," I answered.

Moments after I hung up the phone, another call came through.

"Hello?" I said.

"Hello, this is Harry. I'm interested in the cabin you have advertised. I'd like to come see it."

Puzzled, I rubbed my temples. *Another call about my cabin?*

"Sure, Harry," I said. "You're welcome to come see it, but there are two other people interested in it right now."

Harry took down the directions to my place anyway, and we hung up.

Fifteen minutes later, my daughter called. "Mom, someone just drove into our yard."

"That must be Victor," I mumbled. I walked outside and found a short, heavyset man with small, round glasses framing a balding head. I showed him the cabin.

"Yes, I like this," Victor nodded. He wandered around the outside of the cabin, then stopped and stuck a dull knife into a piece of the trim.

"Aw. . .see, this means wood rot."

"Actually," I responded, "that doesn't reflect the rest of the cabin, because it's just an old piece of wood my husband used to replace part of the original trim."

"Well, you should go down in price," he muttered. "See what Suzy wants to do, then let me know, okay?"

I agreed. He left.

I walked back into the house to see if Suzy had phoned. Still nothing. So I left another message on her answering machine.

"Suzy, please call me right away!"

When I hung up the phone, another message waited for me on my answering machine.

"Hi, my name is Ray. I just saw your ad for the cabin. Please call me back."

I called Ray and explained my dilemma.

"Oh, that's a shame," he said, disappointment ringing in his voice. "But, hey, will you let me know what Suzy decides?"

"Sure," I answered. We said good-bye.

"Mom! Someone else is here!" my son hollered this time as a plump, blond woman wandered toward the cabin.

What's going on here? I wondered, heading toward the door. *Why all this sudden interest in my cabin?* Before I could slip out the door, the phone rang.

"Mom, it's for you."

I rushed back. "Hello?" I answered.

"Hi, this is Suzy. Sorry I never got back to you sooner. Unfortunately, I can't buy the cabin after all."

Well, finally! If only I'd known that from the start, I muttered under my breath. After saying good-bye to Suzy, I scurried out the door to find the blond lady, but she had disappeared. I stood there shaking my head, baffled. Finally, I retreated back into the house and phoned Victor.

"Okay, Victor. I just heard from Suzy. She's not buying the

cabin after all."

"Great!" Victor rejoiced. "I'll take it off your hands for half price."

"Whoa!" I said. "That's too low."

"Well, that's crazy!" he sneered. "You're not going to get a better offer than that."

"Well," I told him. "I'm sure going to try."

We said good-bye, and I laid my head down on the table.

Oh, God, please help me!

Suddenly, I remembered that I was supposed to call Ray, so I scurried over to the phone and dialed him up.

"Hi, Ray. Suzy isn't buying the cabin after all, so you're welcome to come see it."

"Oh, that's wonderful!" he exclaimed. "I'll be right over."

Twenty minutes ticked by and my son called again. "Mom! Now there's a man outside."

I dashed out the door. "Hi, you must be Ray?"

"No, I'm Harry," he answered. "Why? Is someone else coming to look at the cabin?" Harry's eyes grew large and frantic, and I had to fight from laughing because with his thick, disheveled head of brown hair, and short, bushy beard, he looked like a wild jungle man.

"Well," I paused. "Yes, there is."

"Oh, no!" Harry wailed. "My boss sent me here. She was here earlier but left to go get her husband. She wants the cabin."

Good grief! I panicked. *How was I to know? The woman left without saying anything, and now I've invited Ray to come see it.*

Suddenly, a white truck turned onto our graveled driveway.

"Is that your boss?" I asked Harry.

Harry's eyes grew even larger. "No!" he gasped. "That's the other guy, isn't it?"

"Uh, I guess so." I winced.

In a rush, Harry grabbed his cell phone and punched in a number. Then he reached for a wad of money and shoved it at me. "Take this," he pleaded.

I stepped back without taking it. *I'm no salesman!* I screamed in my head. *Shouldn't Ray at least get a chance to see the cabin since I invited him to come?*

Clutching the phone close to his ear, Harry muttered to himself over and over again. "It's mine, it's mine. I was here first."

Oh! If only I could escape this madness.

When Ray climbed out of his truck, I led him to the cabin while Harry looked on in horror. My legs felt weak.

"I'll be in the house if you have any questions," I told Ray in a shaky voice.

Somehow I made it through the door and collapsed into a soft, velvet recliner. *What's going on here? Why has this place turned into a madhouse?* Moments later, my daughter said, "Mom, there's a guy at the door."

With unsteady gait, I walked to the door and found Ray standing there with checkbook and pen in hand.

"I'd like to make an offer," he said, giving me an amount.

Oh, Lord, what do I say? Several seconds of awkward silence went by before I found my voice. "Oh, Ray, I'm sorry. I just don't know what to do. You see, as you were driving into the yard, that man out there was frantic. He tried shoving money at me to reserve the cabin until his boss arrived, but I didn't take it since I invited you over, I figured you should at least be given a chance. I thought after seeing it, you might not be interested. Now, I'm at a loss what to do!"

Ray smiled. Oh, how I needed that! "I'll tell you what," he said. "Let Harry make an offer, then you can sell it to the highest bidder."

I took a deep breath. "Thank you," I said in a voice barely audible.

We walked outside. Ray joined his wife and daughter on one side of my sidewalk. Harry, now joined by his boss, her husband, and their two teenage kids, stood on the other side. When I noticed eight pairs of eyes staring at me, I stopped, frozen in my tracks. *I can't do this!* I cried inwardly. My jaw fell open, but no words came out. Suddenly, the crowd roared with laughter.

"You poor girl," someone said. "Bet this has never happened to you before."

I burst into laughter then, too. "No, it hasn't."

Finally, I looked at Harry and said, "These guys made an offer, but I'll give you a chance to make one, too. Then the highest bidder can have it."

"We'll pay the full asking price," someone from Harry's group piped up.

I glanced over at Ray. "That's all right," he smiled. "Let them have it."

While Harry's boss wrote me a check and made arrangements for pickup, Ray wandered around the acreage. When Harry's group left, I walked over to Ray.

"Are you selling your garden shed?" he asked.

"Yes," I answered.

"Well, I'd like to purchase it, plus your other buildings and fencing."

After Ray left, I sat down on an old log, stunned. *How could so much happen in one afternoon? A hard-to-reach woman, a pompous man, a mysterious woman, a crazy guy, a gentleman, and a clueless saleslady. What a comedy act!* I shook my head in disbelief. Suddenly, a firm yet gentle voice boomed into my thoughts. *NOW DO YOU BELIEVE I CAN STILL MAKE MIRACLES HAPPEN?*

I turned but saw no one. Then as a rush of warmth surrounded me, a smile broke across my face.

"Oh, yes, God, I do!" I laughed. "Thank You for showing me that You really are still in control."

Heavenly
Gifts

God's gifts put man's
best dreams to shame.

Elizabeth Barrett Browning

Don't you love shopping for gifts for friends? It's such a blast to pick out "that special something" for someone you love. When you know someone really well, you know his likes and dislikes, which makes picking out presents even easier. You know if he prefers brown over blue, or quirky over serious. You know if he prefers electronics or tools. Sometimes, if you're really paying attention to the little things a friend says in passing, you know the perfect gift to give. . .just the thing to let him know you care. And when you give it at just the right time, he might think it's ironic, but you will know it's really just a matter of paying attention.

Think about how well our heavenly Father knows us. He not only knows our likes and dislikes, He knows why we feel the way we do about those things. He created us, after all! And when it comes to giving us special gifts, He's the best! God knows exactly what we need. . .when we need it. He makes sure we have "just enough, and just in time." Sometimes He goes the extra mile, giving us extra-special surprises, just so we know He's paying attention to the details.

When was the last time God gave you an extra-special surprise? How did it make you feel? Doesn't it feel great to know He's paying attention and cares enough to bless you in extra-special ways? If so, then imagine how great your friends will feel if they realize you're paying attention to their needs and wants.

So, why not do that? Spend the next few days paying close attention to your friends and family members. Then surprise them with carefully thought-out gifts. Oh, they don't have to be costly. Someone might just need a humorous greeting card. Another would be tickled to get an invitation to dinner. Still another might need a babysitter so that she can have an evening away from the kids. Someone else might need a bag of groceries or a tank of gas. As each gift passes through your fingers, see yourself as a heavenly conduit. Indeed, that present, large or small, is really a heavenly hug from God Himself. He's just using you to accomplish it!

Yes, if you're paying attention, those special love offerings can abound. But giver, beware! We talked about God's boomerang method of blessing earlier. If you're pouring yourself out on behalf of your loved ones, God is sure to shower down blessings on you, too!

For he says, "In the time of my favor I heard you,
and in the day of salvation I helped you." I tell you,
now is the time of God's favor, now is the day of salvation.

2 CORINTHIANS 6:2 NIV

Boiled Peanuts
at Midnight

By Valorie Quesenberry

It had seemed like such a good idea back home in
Sumner. An offer to spend the year in London, doing
research for the Georgia Historical Society—all expenses
paid with some sightseeing thrown in for good measure.
Jaelynn could still hear Aunt Adele gushing.

"My word, child, what an opportuni–ta! I know your
mama and daddy are so proud!" They had been sitting on
the front porch drinking glasses of sweet tea on a hazy afternoon. The heat was smothering, but the high ceiling helped
and the vintage wicker fans were keeping the air stirring.

The house had been in the family for "nigh onto seventy-
five years," as Aunt Adele put it. Countless family reunions
and celebrations and even wakes had ended right here, on
the front porch on Sycamore Street. Sometimes they enjoyed
home-churned peach ice cream or chilled watermelon;

sometimes they just watched the cars, indulging in a bit of good-humored gossip about the destinations of their neighbors. There were very few visitors in Sumner, so every one of its 309 residents was fair game for this pastime.

The cicadas buzzed a homey serenade in the dusk as Jaelynn detailed the offer to her family, bursting with excitement over her unexpected blessing. Following her graduate studies at Georgia State, she had been hired by the Georgia Historical Society, which was now giving her this once-in-a-lifetime chance to travel and work. . .on their tab. Her family, passionate about history in general and family heritage in particular, was excited with her. Of course, she should go. After all, it was only for a year, and think what she could see and do and learn along the way. Wouldn't Gramps and Granny Windsor have been proud? After all, they were descended from English aristocracy who had taken their place in the society of plantation owners when America was only an infant country.

So while the moon rose on their sleepy southern town, Jaelynn and her family talked and laughed and dreamed about what the next year would hold for her.

But now as she sat in a cubbyhole in front of a computer with rain pouring outside, she was having a hard time dredging up that same excitement. She loved the work; following trails of historical facts, discovering ties between the known and the unknown—she could immerse herself for hours. But, when the workday ended and it was time to return to her small flat on a London side street, she missed her Georgia roots desperately.

"Nasty day, what?"

Jaelynn looked up to meet the merry eyes of a coworker. Malcolm Pipstreet was classically British. He had sandy hair, a regal nose, a neatly-trimmed mustache, and a dapper attitude. He didn't look a bit of his fifty-five years. He claimed a Yorkshire terrier and a parakeet as house companions. And contrary to the longstanding joke about the English, he possessed a ready wit and could have her smiling in seconds.

"You said it. At home, we would call this a gully-washer."

Malcolm leaned his elbows on the divider of her cubby. "I say, that's a delightful way to put it. Rather a bit more colorful than simply a rainstorm. Dreadful weather, all the same."

"But I thought Londoners were used to rain?"

"Rain, yes, my dear. But not this tempest brewing outside." He gestured to the window where lightning jagged the sky. "I think I shall spend the evening by the fire with the poet for company."

She grinned. "Shelley or Keats?"

"Possibly Shakespeare. Good for the mind; none of this frothy fiction." He tapped his pencil on the novel lying on her desk and walked off.

In spite of her melancholy, Jaelynn smiled. She so enjoyed their friendly banter.

She clicked the mouse to open the next file on the menu. It was a particularly interesting topic—"Letters to England from the South during the War of Northern Aggression." Jaelynn could see Southern fingerprints all over this file; only folks from Dixie used that title for the Civil War.

She grabbed her coffee mug and sat back to read.

February, 1865
Dearest Corlene,

I take my pen in hand to inform you of my health and recent activities. I suppose you hear news of the war there in Berkshire, but I wonder if they truly report the dreadful facts as they are.

Since my John joined the ranks to defend our beloved South, I have been staying on the plantation with Father, here in Macon. The children and I are well. Susan and Delia amuse themselves with play, serving tea to their dolls with the same china set you and I used as girls. Little Johnny found pieces of a bedraggled Confederate uniform somewhere and finds great pleasure in dressing "as a soldier like Papa," as he says. Though I don't mind his bent to adventure, I shudder to imagine my son experiencing the horrors of the battlefield.

Father does well. He visits Mother's grave daily, somehow managing to find a fresh flower to bring with him.

Jolie still runs the kitchen here, and her cornbread and butter beans are as wondrous as ever. I am grateful that the larder at Heatherton is still giving to us. That is a great testament to the abundance of last year's harvest as well as the ingenuity of Father in concealing our supplies from that plundering hoard of Yankees led by General Sherman.

Oh, Corlene, I cannot find the words to describe to you the absolute destruction left in his wake! Many estates of our friends and neighbors are lying in ruin, their stately pillars crumbling and scorched by fire. The fields are barren as if a swarm of locusts had descended in rage upon them. The towns are pitiful and little children are starving and their mothers have descended so low as to butcher anything that moves upon the ground to keep them alive until their fathers return in glory.

Anymore, I wonder what glory there shall be left for us, dear sister. All that I should ask would be the glory of seeing my John alive and well and knowing that never again shall I fear for my children's lives as we cower in a dank root cellar.

Yet, we fare far better than many. We have tried to be generous as we can, but if the masses know of our remaining food, we should be swarmed with the hungry and I fear then for the lives of any.

I hear that the soldiers have taken to eating peanuts in great quantity. With the fields burned, food for our brave men is scarce. In peanuts, they have found a ready source for their appetite. They have even taken to eating the goobers boiled over a fire with a bit of salted meat thrown in for flavor.

Naturally, I thought of you and our cooking experiments as girls. We still have a goodly portion of peanuts here at Heatherton, so I had Jolie boil some up with a bit of our salt. I must tell you, Corlene, that I was quite dubious of the taste, as privation could cause soldiers to prevaricate about the goodness of their diet. To my surprise, I found that I quite liked them. The shells become soft so they can be opened easily. Their taste reminds me of the pinto beans we often have with cornpone. And the salt gives the whole experience a pleasurable dimension. I wonder if my John is now eating them, too. The other day I heard our soldiers referred to as "goober grabbers." May God have pity on them; they are such brave men.

I have enclosed a small package of our dry Georgia peanuts with this letter, Corlene. Though you are in the land of abundance with our Aunt Josephine and have ample nutrition, I wanted to send you a gift to remind you of your great Southern heritage. You may boil them in some brine and try this new dish that has become a staple here at home. I await your opinion with anticipation.

Write when you can. The winter days are long, though spring approaches soon. We hope to quickly see an end to this conflict and a return to the former days of peace and prosperity.

May God keep you, dearest sister.

Lovingly, Emma

Jaelynn's coffee had grown cold, but she took a reflexive taste anyway. The letter was amazing—such insight into the Civil War era as well as being particularly pleasing to her with Georgia being her home state.

She grabbed a pencil and legal pad to jot down initial thoughts for later research. She felt a sense of kinship with these sisters, one so far from home and in England, no less.

The time on her desk clock read five minutes until closing. She put her notebook into a drawer, arranged the items on her desk, and powered down her work computer. In the morning, she would do an advanced search of the files to find any other letters from Emma Heatherton Cooper.

On the way home, Jaelynn stopped at a marvelous little shop for fish and chips (such an odd name for french fries). She found a table in the corner and listened to the voices around her as she ate. She had discovered that no matter which side of the ocean one was on, people and relationships and families were basically the same. The cultures were different, but under the skin, everyone had needs and fears, joys and triumphs. It reminded her of the last sermon she had heard Pastor Tredell preach before she left home. One particular part was imprinted in her memory.

"This world belongs to our God, every inch. The people in it are His creation and no matter where we are, we are within view of His loving eye and hand of mercy. He is everywhere."

She was sure he spoke the truth.

Jaelynn left the shop and headed for the tube station. Riding on London's subway system was so intriguing for a history buff. It was in these underground caverns that Londoners hid while Nazi bombers ravaged their city. She thought of it every time she stepped into a train for her commute.

Her flat was on Wellington Drive, a typical British street. In the foyer of the weathered stone building, there was a tall brass container for umbrellas, that ubiquitous accessory of every good Londoner. She placed her own flowered one in it. There was a code among the residents—a person's umbrella was sacred property; it was never stolen.

Jaelynn started toward the lift entrance (it even sounded normal now to use that word for the elevator). Passing the row of mailboxes, she noticed a package in her mail space. She pulled it out, surprised as its weight. The return address was Atlanta, Georgia, United States. All the way to the second floor, she tried to guess its contents.

Inside her flat, Jaelynn kicked off her shoes, sank into a chintz armchair, and opened the package. A letter fell out. It was from her sister, Jocelyn.

Dear Jae,

I imagine you're tired after a day's work of research. Knowing you, you're probably putting in extra hours most days. I'm so happy that you are doing what you love, but I miss you terribly. Weekends at home in Sumner just aren't the same without you. Aunt Adele says that when you left the "light went right out of Dixie." I guess I'd have to agree.

*I won't go on very long since I can write longer letters by
e-mail than longhand. (Wouldn't Miss Prentiss from Sumner
High have a fit about my cursive?) But I wanted to send you
a taste of home and had to put a note in with it. I've figured
up the travel time and think you should be getting this by
Thursday. I hope it's not too heavy to carry to your room. The
canned ones aren't nearly as good as the fresh ones from Hill's
Farm Stand, but they'll have to do. I know how much you
love them.*

*I'll be having some myself for the next few nights, probably
around at 8:00 when I'm done with the evening routine here at
the library. If you want to join me, we'll call this a long-distance
sisterly snack, okay?*

Much love always,

Jocie

*P.S. At home last weekend, I found something you should
research. Mama gave me a packet of letters to an Emma
Heatherton Cooper, an ancestor of ours. It seems she had a sister
in England, too, at one point. Thought you might run across
something about her. Let me know.*

Jaelynn pulled back the packaging to reveal ten cans of
boiled peanuts. It must have cost Jocelyn a fortune to send
something so heavy.

She held one up to her cheek. "Thanks, sis. What a
perfect gift."

The time difference between London and Georgia meant that 8:00 p.m. in Atlanta would be 12:00 a.m. here. Who cared? That would give her time to do some further research on her laptop about Emma Heatherton Cooper. Just wait until she told Jocelyn about that coincidence. In fact, it wouldn't surprise her at all to discover that Emma and Corlene had also shared a long-distance sisterly snack like she and Jocelyn. And Jaelynn was sure that nothing would taste any better to two sisters than boiled peanuts at midnight.

Those Crazy
Coincidences

Coincidence is God's way
of remaining anonymous.

ALBERT EINSTEIN

When you hear someone use the words, "Wow, that was an amazing coincidence!" how do you respond? The word "coincidence" isn't an easy one to define, but it helps to look at the root words. It comes from the Latin: *cum-* (which means "with" or "together") and *incidere*, (which basically means "to happen"). Combine those and you get "to happen with" or "to happen together." The most interesting definition of all is a scientific one. In science, a "coincidence" occurs when two rays of light strike a surface at the same point. . .at the same time. [1]

What are the chances? Pretty slim, right?

Those of us who put our trust in God realize that most of the things that look like coincidences (two or more events happening "by chance") are really God-incidences. Sure, some things seem improbable—say, waking up at three in the morning with the distinct urge to pray for a good friend, only to find out later that she barely escaped being in an accident at that very same moment. But, remember. . .we serve a God of the improbable. In fact, He's referred to in scripture as a God of the impossible. So, if the impossible is possible to Him, then the improbable (God-incidences) shouldn't surprise us at all! They're just part of the package.

God-incidences serve many purposes in our lives. Primarily, they let us know that we're not alone. In other words, they're just another one of God's heavenly XOXOs!

1   http://en.wikipedia.org/wiki/Coincidence

His handiwork is all around us, and none of it is happening "by chance."

Just about the time we feel no one is paying attention—that we have no significance at all—along comes a personalized "coincidence," and we're startled back to reality. Something—or rather, Someone—far greater is in control. And apparently He's got a pretty good handle on the details of our lives! When we see Him move in such a miraculous way, we know He can be trusted to take care of us in good times and in bad.

The Bible says that we are fearfully and wonderfully made. God's hand is on you, and His heart is with you. How then, could anything happen by accident? He cares about you too much for that! So the next time something "coincidental" happens, you can rest assured, God was behind it. No one knows you better than He does. And isn't it fun to watch Him prove it?

"God-incidences" might seem improbable. They might even seem impossible. But they happen every day, and each one delights the heart of God. So, be on the lookout! Could be, a God-incidence is on the way!

"For nothing will be impossible with God."

LUKE 1:37 NASB

Coincidence

By Paul Muckley

D o you believe in coincidence?

Before you answer, consider this story of a new family and a used van. The story is 100 percent true—only the names have been changed, as they say, to protect the innocent.

Self-assessment would have plopped Lynne and me squarely into the "young couple" category. But we weren't really *that* young—she was thirty-two, I was thirty-three. Married for nine years, we only heard the pitter-patter of little feet at home when our two cats were on the prowl.

Of course, we wanted kids. But the doctor could never pinpoint why they didn't come. Officially, we were experiencing an "unexplained infertility."

The good news was that it wasn't my fault, nor was it Lynne's. But that little pat on the back didn't put a baby in the nursery. Fertility treatments followed, though only for a few frustrating and expensive months. Adoption, always a hazy possibility, soon sharpened into our preferred option.

Lynne and I are both white, but when we learned that the agency we'd chosen wanted prospective parents for its "transracial" program, we quickly signed on for any biracial baby that might come along. And, relatively quickly, one did. We learned about Hialeah a little more than a week before she was due.

Our "nine-day pregnancy" flew by, a week and two days of mad scrambling to prepare a nursery and buy baby clothes, diapers, bottles, medicines—you name it. For a while, we felt like we were single-handedly pushing the national economy in a nifty new stroller.

And then came the phone call—our baby had been born!

Most nights are far too short. This one felt like a year. But the morning finally arrived, and we were soon making a ninety-minute drive to the hospital to meet our birth mom, Kelsey. Hialeah was resting in the neonatal intensive care unit while doctors observed a breathing problem. If all went well with Kelsey, we'd get to see the baby later that day.

Things went very well. Kelsey was a quiet, serious young woman in her early twenties, and we felt a quick connection with her. Her upbringing had been far less than ideal, but she was trying to make something of her life by enrolling in classes at a nearby community college. Kelsey was hoping, someday, to be a professional chef.

She already had a three-year-old daughter, Aria, and knew it would be very difficult to handle a second baby on her own. As with every good mom, Kelsey wanted a better opportunity for Hialeah, and—excruciating as the decision was for her—knew she had to place the baby up for adoption.

Our visit lasted more than two hours. We talked about where we'd all come from and where we hoped to go in life. We discussed our parenting philosophies and our plans for our families. We soon felt like old friends.

And then Kelsey made the announcement that would literally change our lives: She wanted *us* to parent Hialeah.

So it was finally time to meet this kid.

Kelsey, Lynne, and I walked together to the NICU. It was a serious place, with some gravely ill babies fighting for their health—and in some cases, their lives—amid brightly colored decorations put up by the nursing staff. Though Hialeah had problems, they weren't considered life threatening.

A nurse pointed us to Hialeah's area. There, partially hidden by breathing tubes, monitor wires, and the plastic cover of her sterile bassinet, lay the most beautiful baby we'd ever seen. Her cocoa skin and shock of shiny dark hair literally took my breath away—a quick gasp, followed by the conscious decision to breathe again. And that was before I'd even caught my first glimpse of her stunning brown eyes.

Call it a cliché, but there was magic in the air. And there was magic in our first touch, even if that came through a rubber glove attached to the bassinet cover. Hialeah's heartbeat and breathing were racing, as we could clearly see on the monitor over her bed. But they each calmed dramatically when I laid my hand on her little body.

Hialeah spent a week in that hospital, and so did Lynne. The medical staff allowed Lynne to stay in a small dormlike room that had once housed nursing students, so she could both learn the care of a newborn and help out with the same.

My employer, a book publisher, gave me freedom to come and go as needed that week, so I generally worked until early afternoon then drove an hour and a half to visit "my girls." Lynne was holding, feeding, and changing Hialeah each day, and as the week went on, I did, too. And I found that diapers weren't quite as frightening as I'd earlier thought.

Hialeah grew stronger and stronger, slowly but surely shedding the various wires and tubes she'd been sporting. I was most pleased when the nurses finally removed an intravenous line stuck directly into our daughter's forehead.

When the doctor announced that we could take Hialeah home the next day, it struck me that we still needed a baby seat for the car. That was easily enough remedied at the big-box baby store on the way home, which happened to be holding a baby-seat safety check that day. You can bet those checkers heard the whole story of our little girl!

I returned to the hospital the next morning, on a very chilly late September day. We thanked the nurses and said good-bye. We thanked Kelsey—though that seemed pitifully inadequate for the gift she'd given us—and said good-bye. And we carried Hialeah in her brand-new punkin seat to our little blue Chevy Cavalier, legally waiting in the "patient pick-up" lane.

If you're familiar with vehicle makes, you'll recognize the Cavalier as a "compact car." That means it's small. And our two-door model posed a few challenges to situating a baby carrier in the cramped backseat.

We worked with that for a while, but it didn't take long for all the head-bumpings and back-wrenchings to get us thinking about a more family-friendly vehicle. Now what says "family" more than a minivan? We started visiting used car lots in search of a vehicle upgrade.

Before long, a green Dodge Caravan caught Lynne's eye. It *was* pretty sharp—with paint stripes and body skirting that made it much sportier than most of its minivan cousins. It was definitely used, with eighty-some thousand miles under its frame. But the price was right, and we knew we could grow into the vehicle. Hialeah was never intended to be an only child.

Financing came through the Bank of Mom—Lynne's mom, who withdrew some cash out of a retirement account. Our plan was to pay her back as quickly as possible, starting with whatever we received in a royalty check, due in about five months.

I've mentioned my job with a book publisher. As an editor, I would generally pass judgment on other people's writing—as proposals that arrive through the mail or as manuscripts that I've contracted and received from authors. But a couple of years earlier, I'd jumped the fence and obtained a contract for a book of my own. Not the great American novel, but a book of Bible trivia. Though we never expected that book to make us rich, Lynne and I did plan to put the income it generated toward building our family. And stepping up from a tiny car to a van was one part of that plan.

My book was relatively small and inexpensive, the royalty rate modest. Averaged over all the various sales channels, each copy sold would yield roughly a dime.

But God was good and the book was popular. In its first year, more than two hundred thousand copies sold, and the resulting royalty—a little over twenty thousand dollars—covered the costs of Hialeah's adoption. Believe me, we were thankful. In the early years of our marriage, finding several thousand dollars for an adoption would have been more than daunting—it would have been nearly impossible.

But those days were behind us now. We'd brought Hialeah into our home, finalized the adoption in court at the six-month mark, and thrilled to every tiny thing she learned and did. If you have kids, you know what I mean—all those things that every baby on earth learns and does, but that seem utterly miraculous when they happen to yours.

Since she was able to stay home with Hialeah, Lynne saw almost everything first—the first time the baby rolled over, the first time she sat by herself, the first time she ate solid food. But I like to claim Hialeah's first real smile.

Maybe she appreciated me as the family's provider. I kept on editing books, critiquing others' writing while casting an occasional eye over the sales of my own. That Bible trivia kept selling, and those dimes kept adding up. Not long after Hialeah's first professional portrait at five months, my annual book accounting would come due.

Generally, the skill sets of editors and accountants don't overlap very much, and that was certainly true in my case. I had only a very rough idea of what payment to expect, and hoped—without any real evidence—that it would be large enough to pay off our entire van loan at once.

Royalty reports carry all kinds of information—like the number of copies sold, to which markets, at what discounts, before how many returns come back to the publisher's warehouse. But my guess is that ninety-nine out of every one hundred writers look immediately to a single section of the printout, the one that reads "Total earnings this period." I know that's where I always went first.

Would it be enough to retire the loan?

Let's see. . .

$10,644.04.

Hey, cool. . .it is enough!

But, wait a minute. . .

Why does that number seem so familiar?

Ten thousand, six hundred forty-four.

I know I've seen that number somewhere before.

Hmmm. . .

No way. . .

Could it be?

Downstairs to the old metal filing cabinet, and pull out the top drawer—the one that screeches horribly ever since the little plastic rollers fell off. Thumb though the folders and grab the one labeled "Automotive."

Inside, there's a bill of sale for our green Dodge Caravan. Sale price, tax, title, and all other expenses total—you guessed it—$10,644.00.

Coincidence?

Not in our minds. We prefer to think of that as a God-thing.

Now, some people might quibble over the additional four cents on the royalty check. If it's really a God-thing, why wouldn't those figures be exact to the penny?

But we chose not to worry over that.

The spare change went into Hialeah's college savings account.

9

A Life Poured Out

Angels descending,
bring from above,
echoes of mercy,
whispers of love.

FANNY J. CROSBY

Likely you've read the scripture: "Greater love has no one than this: to lay down one's life for one's friends" (John 15:13 NIV). It's one of those scriptures that mesmerizes and perplexes most of us. It can also scare the daylights out of us! After all, we're talking about the supreme sacrifice here.

Or are we?

To lay down our lives doesn't necessarily mean the shedding of blood. Oftentimes it just means that we need to be more invested in the lives of others, expecting nothing in return. When we invest in the lives of our friends—when we're really paying attention to their trials and tribulations— we're more likely to see their needs and give accordingly. . . of our time, our efforts, and our money. We're willing to go above and beyond because we love them so much.

But what about those outside our tight circle? Aren't all our brothers and sisters across the globe our "friends"? If so, is God asking us to give more than just a passing glance to those in need far from where we live and worship? This is where we start to get nervous. After all, it's one thing to lay down your life for someone you love. Can you imagine doing so for people on the other side of the planet that you've never even met?

God longs for us to be His hands extended, not just to hurting people in our neighborhoods or states, but across the globe. Starving children in Africa should be our priority. Earthquake victims in Haiti must be on our minds.

Struggling missionaries in Ecuador depend on us for help. House church leaders in China are relying on us to pray. All of those around the planet who are in need are counting on us to play a role. And we must! We need to open both our pocketbooks and our hearts to them, and lay down our very lives—financially and otherwise.

"To people I've never even met?" you might ask. Yes! This is God's plan, after all.

So, how do you feel about this global vision? Does it scare you? Instead of feeling overwhelmed, feeling you must help everyone, why not choose one ministry or group, and send a monthly support check? If you can't do that, then focus your prayers on this group and its participants. The ultimate goal here is to feel connected to our brothers and sisters in Christ who are ministering for the sake of the gospel.

Laying down our lives. . .it's a challenge, to be sure. But it's one we can meet with a smile.

"Give, and it will be given to you. A good measure, pressed down, shaken together and running over, will be poured into your lap. For with the measure you use, it will be measured to you."

LUKE 6:38 NIV

The Angel
of Bosnia

BY DAVID MCLAUGHLAN

When I set out with the children that day, I wasn't
looking for angels.

We were on holiday in the north of England and staying
by a particularly impressive stretch of coast. When the
tide was out, you could see a series of giant circular pat-
terns in the rock. I'm sure there is a geological explanation
for them but, and far as the kids and I were concerned,
as we looked down from the cliff top, it looked like God
Himself had stuck His finger in the molten rock and
swirled it around.

The previous year, when I had last been in the area, I had
found an interesting but old and abandoned structure near
the edge of the cliffs. Two stories high, it was a tall concrete
box with big, unglazed windows looking out to the sea. The
remains of a balcony ran around three of the walls.

I had thought eleven-year-old Amy and ten-year-old Josh might like to explore it, (carefully, of course). But when we got there things had changed dramatically. The balcony had been rebuilt, the windows were glazed, there was a flag flying from the roof, and there was a man up there peering out to sea through a pair of binoculars.

Coming closer we saw a table arranged outside the building. Second-hand books and homemade bookmarks were for sale—a fundraiser for a group called Sea-watch. There was also a laminated invitation to climb the ladder by the side wall and visit.

"Do you want to?" I challenged the kids.

"Do *you* want to?" they replied, nervously.

"Come on." I laughed. "Let's go!"

The Sea-watch guys were great. They made the children feel welcome, and they were only too happy to answer my questions.

The tower had been built during World War II. Looking out across the North Sea it was manned by the Home Guard in an attempt to spot any possible enemy incursions. Thankfully, none came that way, and it was soon abandoned. The Coast Guard used it for a while. Now this voluntary group occupied it. They were a reference point and information station for tourists. They handed out sunscreen and warned about tides and dangerous currents. They looked out for boats in trouble and passed information to the police about the occasional smuggling that went on in the area.

As a way to spend some of your retirement years, I thought, *I have seen a lot worse.*

One of the guys, though, seemed a little different from the rest. His military background was given away by his bearing—oh, and the fact that the other men referred to him as "the major."

At the time I was writing articles for magazines and was always on the lookout for a good story. After hearing a thing or two that piqued my interest, I asked if I might be able to come back some time and interview him. He agreed, but the children weren't so obliging.

"Why not do it now?" Amy asked.

The major laughed and shrugged. The sea was quiet, and he did like to tell his story! Josh and Amy climbed onto the swivel chairs by the window, and, recognizing I was outnumbered, I gave in gracefully. I took out my notepad and began scribbling like mad to keep up with the major's tale of wonder.

Service was deeply rooted in this man. After a career as "something in the military" and a short stint in the priesthood, he had retired to the northeast coast, but not to sit with his feet up. So, after discovering the abandoned watchtower, he rustled up some like-minded souls, found funding, and set up Sea-watch.

Having escaped Saigon just before the fall (by paying "thousands" to get out of the country), the Major and his wife arrived in England with just over fifteen dollars between them. Needing a change of direction and wanting to get away from the military, he headed for the priesthood.

At around the same time Czechoslovakia fell apart and the Bosnian war broke out, the Major was conducting a service at Oxford University chapel with a colleague who would later go on to become the Queen's chaplain.

"There was a girl crying her eyes out in the church," he told us. "Her father was a Serbian and her mother a Croat, and she said to me, 'Would you help us?'

"I said, 'Yes.' And she said, 'In front of Jesus, swear an oath!' So, I did.

"My colleague offered to take the service, and I turned away to make us some coffee. When I turned back, she was gone. My colleague said she hadn't left past him. But there wasn't another way out. Not usually a man to comment on such things, he just couldn't get over how beautiful she had been. When I told him about the oath, I'd been surprised to find I had just made, he said, 'Well. . .you better do something about it then, hadn't you.'

"So, I went on TV and said we'd be sending two truckloads of aid to Bosnia. I didn't know how to get permits. I didn't know how to get trucks. I had no idea how to get supplies! But in fourteen days we had twenty-one tons of aid ready to go. We had five drivers. They got shot up a bit. . . ."

The memory of these attacks on people only trying to help sobered him for a moment.

"Then I got a call from the Croatian Embassy, which then consisted of one room. They needed supplies for a maternity hospital. It just so happened I had a visitor in the church at that very moment who knew who to ask. I rang them, and within twenty-four hours they got thousands of those specific supplies from Edinburgh to us in Cambridge. They were then flown out to Zagreb and were being used within forty-eight hours of that request being made.

"We had a call from the Shetland Isles, offering forty tons of educational materials. How were we going to get it from the Shetlands, far off the north coast of Scotland, to Oxford in the south of England? Well, amazingly, the German navy brought it down to us for free!

"Things just seemed to happen like that! Funny things happened as well. A chap rang up asking if we would like some gripe water used to settle babies' stomachs. We thought it might be a box of bottles. He sent us ninety-six thousand bottles of the stuff. There were a lot of burping babies in those Bosnian, Slovenian, and Croatian hospitals when that delivery arrived!

"In two years we shipped a thousand tons. In five years, another six thousand. By now my career in the church had taken a distant second place to helping the Bosnian people."

I commented on how inspirational the people he worked with must have been and could only wonder how this must have contrasted with the horrors other men perpetrated.

"Yup! I visited one camp of seven hundred women whose husbands had all been murdered. We're only on this earth a short time. Why can't we just get along?"

When the major closed his operation down, he had letters of thanks from thirteen ambassadors and two heads of state. But this was dismissed with a wave of the hand. For the major it was all about the people.

"Oh, we'll never be rich," he said, "but I've helped people, and I can live with that."

By the end of the operation, his doctor suggested his health had suffered.

"Well," he explained, "we were always getting calls in the middle of the night, and I could never say no. You would get the ambassador of one country saying, 'We need a planeload for a hospital,' or someone else would need help in another country. It got so I couldn't sleep and my nerves were shattered."

Taking a shipment of aid to a port on the English Channel for shipping to Europe and knowing the lifetime organization of a hardy band of volunteers was coming to an end, he spotted a group doing voluntary work along that stretch of coast and decided he could do something similar in the northeast. And so, Sea-watch came into being.

At the first meeting, he had four volunteers turn up. The police and local authority told him he was wasting his time. "But that kind of response only makes me more determined.

"The first winter we had no doors and no windows. We all got the flu. But the word spread, and it really took off."

He regaled us with some of the things that had happened over the years. He'd pulled someone's sinking car from the sands using his own car as a tow truck. The fellow had said, "Thank you very much," and drove off. The major had to pay fifteen hundred pounds to get his own car repaired afterward. They made welcome a group of four hundred city kids who had never been to the seaside before. He had taken a group of visitors on a moonlit night hike along the cliff tops when they heard some desperate voices. Two elderly ladies, stopping for the night on their way to London, had decided to take their dogs for an evening stroll on the sands. They had been cut off. Backed against the cliffs by the rising tide, they had no option but to scream for help and hope someone heard.

Those ladies, like so many other people, had cause to be glad that the major was around.

Well, the story seemed to be coming to an end. My hand was cramping from taking notes. The children had sat, engrossed through most of it, but now those swivel chairs were swiveling more and more toward the spectacular view out the windows.

We talked a little about his plans to expand Sea-watch into other coastal areas. I told him how impressed I was with all his work and thanked him for his time.

Like a gentleman, he climbed down the ladder first, just in case the children slipped. I put a contribution in the collection tin and shook his hand warmly. It had been a genuine pleasure to meet this extraordinary man.

As I was about to turn away and walk back to the hotel, I remembered the girl in the church, that extraordinarily beautiful young woman who belonged to both sides of a war.

Since the major kept his promise to her, everything seemed to have fallen into place. Her tears had generated a major humanitarian movement. An obvious idea occurred to me, but I hesitated to put it into words.

Seeing my consternation the major asked, "Was there something else?"

I put my embarrassment aside and asked, "Do you think she could have been an angel? That girl in the church."

It obviously wasn't the first time the idea had crossed his mind, but he stuck his jaw out defiantly. "I don't believe in that sort of thing anymore," he said flatly. "I find it hard to see God in some of the things I've seen."

I was temporarily at a loss for something to say. Then my daughter filled the gap. I don't know if this was something she had heard in Sunday school or something that had just occurred to her, but it was the perfect thing to say.

"Maybe if you didn't see God, it was because He was behind you, pushing you in the right direction."

The silence that followed was broken only by the wind and the seagulls. Then the major smiled at my daughter.

"The older I get," he said slowly, "the more I think that just might be true."

It was a moment that could only be described as "hopeful" all round.

The Friendship Factor

True friends are hard to find,
difficult to leave,
and impossible to forget.

AMANDA KUNKLE

Perhaps you've heard the old expression that some friendships are for a season, and others are for a reason. Likely we've all had a few friendships over the years that seemed as brief as a candle's flicker. Those friends came and went from our lives very quickly. They were only there for a brief season before life's circumstances changed. Then they moved on, and we never heard from them again. Still, they made a dramatic impact on us in a short period of time, changing us in a host of ways.

Other friends are there because they've been sent from God to minister to us in some way, or vice versa. They have the uncanny ability to know when we're hurting, even if we haven't vocalized our pain. And they're amazing prayer warriors. They're the ones we go to with the big stuff. We know in our heart of hearts that life would be much tougher without them.

Some friends, of course, are lifers. They're meant to stick with us. . .forever. With these friends, we fall into easy, comfortable relationship. They're like a pair of worn slippers, familiar and cozy, comfy and reliable. For these, we are eternally grateful.

It's probably for the best that we don't know God's motivation for linking us with our friends from the get-go. If we knew that our new best friend was only going to live nearby for another two or three years, it might put a damper on things. And if we knew that a friend at work was placed in the cubicle next to us to reach out to us after losing a parent or child, it would certainly change the dynamic of the relationship from the onset.

No, it's for the best that we can't see God's logic. But isn't it amazing that He knows just who to place in our lives. . . and when? He knows the people we need and the ones who need us, as well. And He's especially good at using us to express His heart, His love, and His blessings to one another. In other words, we can trust Him to bring the right person at the right time. And we can also trust Him to send us to care for people during their time of need.

As you ponder these things, why not make a list of the friends and loved ones in your life? Begin to seek out new ways to minister to them and to thank them for how they minister to you. And while you're at it, spend some time thanking God for both the privilege of loving. . .and being loved. What a blessing!

"His master replied, 'Well done, good and faithful servant! You have been faithful with a few things; I will put you in charge of many things. Come and share your master's happiness!'"

Matthew 25:23 NIV

A Guest Appearance

By David McLaughlan

We tend to think of the story of our lives as *our* story. Sometimes, though, with the benefit of hindsight and a little emotional distance, we might look back and see the things we thought were all about us were actually more important as part of someone else's story. And maybe that's the way it should be if we are living lives of service.

This story, which I *thought* was mine, began on a rainy winter's evening in Glasgow, Scotland. Standing in Central Station, trying to get home to the coast, I looked up at the display boards and sighed as train after train was first delayed and then cancelled.

I'd been waiting for over two hours to catch one of the trains that normally left every fifteen minutes. The problem was the rain. It was drumming off the roof of the train station, just like it had been all week. Higher level lines were fine, but the railway line that took me and hundreds of others home ran, in part, through a valley. In better weather the valley and the lochs in it were popular with local fishermen, but in wet weather (really wet weather) those lochs rose, burst their banks, and crept upwards to the railway line.

Brave souls had been venturing out to the valley each morning before the first train to see if they would be able to run a service that day. For those of us who had to get to work, the only option was to show up and wait.

Well, I'd gotten to work that day—but might not be getting back home.

Then they announced a train was going to try to get through.

Wrapped in the cocoon of the carriage, the journey didn't seem any different from normal. Once or twice we really slowed down but, looking out the window, all we could see was our reflections refracted in the rain and reflected by the dark.

We pulled into a little station in the middle of the valley. *So far, so good*, I thought. But the train doors didn't open. We just sat there. And sat there. Twenty minutes passed with no announcement. Then the lights went out.

Whatever problems the driver was having kept him distracted for another ten minutes. Then the doors hissed open, and he announced that this train would be returning to Glasgow. Anyone not wanting to return with it should get out now.

A trainload of people disembarked onto the platform. The station was unmanned; the waiting room was closed; people squeezed into the smokers' shelter. Those who couldn't get in were soaked in seconds.

I wasn't going to hang out. I decided to explore the village beside the station. A few minutes later, I saw the lights of a taxi coming out of the dark. I waved him down. Could he take me to a little town called Kilwinning? It was about thirty miles away.

"Take you there?" The bear of a man behind the wheel laughed. "I was born there."

So I jumped in. On an impulse I asked him to drive past the station. Standing a little aside from the main crowd, I saw a young mom trying her best to shelter her baby.

"Where do you live?" I shouted out the window. It was a few miles farther down the road than me. "Jump in," I said. "I don't have any money," she replied. "But I can pay when we get to my house."

Davie, the taxi driver, was a real chatterbox. It turned out he knew my folks. He talked all the way home while the young woman stayed quiet in the backseat. It occurred to me she might have thought she was taking a risk. Perhaps it was a measure of her desperation to get her baby home.

A mile from my place I asked Davie to pull over. I could get out at this junction, and he could take the woman and her baby straight on. It would get her home quicker. I gave him enough money to pay the fare for both of us.

He hesitated, then called me a gentleman and shook my hand.

Well, that's how it all began!

A year later I was married and going to a dance with my wife. Guess which taxi driver turned up to take us there— Davie. I didn't recognize him at first, but he remembered that night and spent the whole trip telling my wife what a righteous fellow I was. He recalled how the woman in the back of his cab had been busy with her baby and hadn't known what I was doing when I got out and how wonderful she thought it was to arrive safely home and find her fare already paid.

I tried my best to steer the conversation onto something else but, hey, it didn't hurt to have my wife know I was a gentleman even when she wasn't there.

The next time I met Davie, it was Christmas Day. A busy time for taxi drivers, and a time when they charge double fare.

Four generations of the family had gathered at my mother's house for a party. Near the end of the evening, we were all well fed and ready to put our feet up. But I had some young family members to get to the next town. I phoned a taxi, and Davie showed up. We wished each other seasons greetings, and I gave him enough cash to cover the fare. When he dropped the youngsters off, he handed them the money back and said it was a Christmas present!

Time and again Davie was our driver. He would insist on giving us a reduced rate. I would insist on giving him more than going rate. It was almost a competition to see who could be the nicest guy.

When he won the argument, I would put on a sour face and say I was going to phone a "real" taxi driver next time. But I never did.

On one of our trips together, I noticed Davie wasn't his usual chatty self. Oh, he still had that big wide-open smile— but it didn't seem to reach as far as his eyes. And there were actual gaps in the conversation. That wasn't like Davie at all. Something was up.

"Acht!" he said, waving a hand as if to wave the whole thing away. "It's just my mother. She's not very well."

I told him I was sorry to hear that. I'd heard Davie talk about his mom several times. He had an almost puppylike adoration for the woman.

"Actually, she's dying." Davie quickly brushed his cheek with the back of his hand. When he turned toward me, the smile was back—but I have never seen a smile so strained. "The doc says she has only days left."

I have no idea how we passed the rest of that trip.

This was a man I only knew in his workplace. But I felt I knew enough about him to know the heart of the man. We were really different guys in lots of ways, but I felt he had the heart of a servant, and I guess he thought the same about me. It was enough on its own to form a bond.

Well, I couldn't get Davie's mom off my mind. I managed to stall for a day, before remembering there weren't any days to spare. I swallowed my embarrassment and gathered my courage.

Davie had mentioned the sheltered housing complex his mom lived in, so I turned up at the reception area with a bunch of flowers. I was tempted to leave them there and run. But I didn't.

The oddness of the situation was reflected in the faces of the staff. Here I was, a guy turning up with flowers for an elderly lady I didn't know and hadn't ever met. I didn't even know her first name.

After checking to make sure it was okay with her, they showed me through to her apartment. A nurse took me into Davie's mom's bedroom.

Oh man, I was so not supposed to be in this lady's room—yet here I was, trying to undo the knot that had formed in my throat.

She looked up from the bed with an honest expression of delight on her face. I looked around the room, desperately trying to think of something to say. Everywhere there were signs of this woman's faith. And there were about a dozen vases full of fresh flowers!

I held my bouquet out and suggested she might have trouble finding space for it. The nurse took it from me and assured me she would find yet another vase.

"Isn't it beautiful," Davie's mom whispered, and I assumed she was talking about the flowers. "I'm going home," she added. And there was Davie's smile.

Well, I felt I ought to introduce myself. "I'm a friend of Davie's," I said. "Well, not a friend. A customer, perhaps." Then I told her the whole story. As I came to the end, I revised my introduction. "Actually," I said, "I *am* a friend of Davie's. He told me you weren't feeling so great. . .and. . .I just wanted to tell you that you raised a son to be proud of."

She seemed to think about this for a while, then she simply said, "Thank you." I stammered that I had better go now, but before I left I did a thing that amazes me even now. I stepped closer, kissed her on the forehead, and said, "God bless."

If I'd put off my visit much longer, I would have been too late. Davie's mom passed away the next day.

The task wasn't complete. There would be a funeral. Would it be too much if I showed up? The man was my taxi driver, for goodness' sake. Would he think it odd for me to turn up at his mother's funeral? Had he heard about the flowers? Did he already think I was weird?

These are the kind of thoughts that are planted in our minds to separate the good in our hearts from this world and the others in it.

Standing awkwardly at the graveside I tried not to be too conspicuous among a bunch of folk I didn't know. Then Davie arrived. Shaking hands and receiving condolences, he cut through the crowd and wrapped me in a bear hug.

He had been with his mum just before she died. And hadn't seen her so happy for a long time. She told him she'd spent her life raising her children, then, at the end of it all, a stranger came along and told her she'd done a good job. "What more," she asked him, "could a mother want?"

And he cried. And I cried.

But, really, it wasn't about either of us. That's the trap lots of people fall into, especially guys. We think our lives are all about us. But this story wasn't about torrential rain, it wasn't about paying taxi fares, it wasn't about which of us could be the nicest guy or the biggest gentleman.

This story was about a character who hardly featured. It was about a little lady who spent her life loving God and raising fine children; a lady who had done what she thought she was put on this world for, and done it with grace. Years in advance, God had set a train of events in motion that put a nervous, confused stranger by her bedside to tell her the equivalent of, "Well done, thou good and faithful servant."

Looking back I now know all that stuff wasn't my story. But I am honored to have been chosen to make a guest appearance in *her* story. And, after all, it would not be the first time God has used a flood to arrange things just the way He wanted them.

Dear Lord, thank You for the many ways You show up in my life. You overwhelm me with Your love and tender mercies. I never cease to be amazed by You. Day in and day out, I sense Your nearness through the circumstances I face, and I'm convinced of Your great affection for me. Oh, how wonderful it feels, to know I'm loved by the Creator of the universe! What can I do but share this love with others? I praise You for that opportunity and thank You in advance for the many wonders yet to come. Your heavenly XOXOs are the best, Lord!

A Final Thought:
Our Unchanging God

What a generous and loving God we serve! He is on the lookout for special ways to bless us, to remind us that He's ever-present, and that He cares. He also longs for us to do His will and bless others, to be His hands extended. Hopefully these stories have stirred you to do just that.

Remember, our God is unchanging. He's the same yesterday, today, and forever. If He took the time to reach out and speak to the great heroes of the faith—Noah, Abraham, David, and so on—we've got to believe He'll do the same for us. Sure, it's overwhelming to think that the Creator of all would take the time to whisper a word of comfort in our ears or arrange a supernatural intervention in our lives, but that's exactly what He plans to do! So, stay on the lookout for heavenly XOXOs. Don't let them catch you unawares.

If you're going through a rough patch, be especially tuned in to what God wants to do. Don't overlook His attempts to connect with you in a special one-on-one way simply because the circumstances aren't ideal. Instead, keep your eyes wide open. Could be, a "God-incidence" is just around the bend. You can rest assured that God is on the move. He always has been. . .and He always will be.

Contributors

Angela Deal graduated from the Institute of Children's Literature writing course in 1997 and is currently an apprentice level student through the Jerry B. Jenkins Christian Writers Guild. She resides in Alberta, Canada, with her husband, Dwain. They have six children between the ages of fourteen and twenty-two. Angela works part time as a commercial janitor and also homeschools her three youngest children. In her spare time, she enjoys reading and writing.

David McLaughlan used to write whatever turned a buck, but now writes about faith and God. It doesn't pay as well— but it does make his heart sing! He lives in bonnie Scotland with Julie and a whole "clan" of children.

Kimm Reid-Matchett is a writer and proud mother of four. With a degree in psychology and the personal experience of being a single mother for many years, she has developed a deep passion for single parents and their children and specializes in single parent family counseling. Kimm is recently remarried and currently lives in Alberta, Canada, where she is founder and president of Grace Enough Ministries.

Charles F. Miller lives in Toledo, Ohio. He taught at Toledo Christian High School, has been a hospital chaplain, and currently works as a surgical tech and freelance writer. He loves Russian and Polish poets, Solzhenitsyn, Lewis, and Tolkien. He has been published in *Dogma* and *Cat Nips* by Katherine Douglas; in *Heavenly Humor for the Dog Lover's Soul* and *Heavenly Humor for the Cat Lover's Soul*, also from Barbour; and in the *Ancient Paths* annual literary anthology.

Paul Muckley lives in eastern Ohio with his wife, Laurie, and three adopted children. Their youngest came with a one-day notice, when Hialeah's birth mother called unexpectedly to ask if they would also adopt her newborn son. (How do you say no to that?) A graduate of Cedarville College in southwest Ohio, Paul has worked with Barbour Publishing since 1998 and now serves as senior editor for nonfiction.

Valorie Bender Quesenberry is a pastor's wife, mother of four, blogger, speaker, and writer. She is the author of two books, *Reflecting Beauty: Embracing the Creator's Design* (Wesleyan Publishing House, 2010) and *Redeeming Romance: Delighting in God's Love* (to release in 2011). Valorie enjoys communicating truth through both fiction and nonfiction.